Also by Barry Friedman

Novels

Dead End

Assignment: Bosnia

Prescription For Death

The Shroud

Sleeper

Hyde

Max

That's Life: It's Sexually Transmitted and Terminal

*The Old Folks at Home: Warehouse Them or Leave
Them on the Ice Floe*

Fracture

Non-Fiction

The Short Life of a Valiant Ship

Barry Friedman

SURVIVOR:

USS Russell a World War Two Destroyer

By

Barry Friedman

Survivor

SURVIVOR:
USS Russell a World War Two Destroyer

ISBN-10: 1475242204
13: 9781475242201

Barry Friedman

DEDICATION

To the men of the fighting *Russell*. They were the best of what Tom Brokaw had in mind when he termed them The Greatest Generation.

And to the men and women of the new *Russell (DDG-59)* who are gallantly upholding the tradition of their namesake.

Survivor

Table of Contents

Barry Friedman

Survivor

Foreword

The history of *USS Russell (DD-414)* is a history of the pre-Pearl Harbor Battle of the Atlantic and of the Pacific War of 1941 to 1945.

In 1995, Robert "Robbie" Robinson, *Russell's* Chief Quartermaster who became a commissioned officer, published a book titled *The Invincible Russell DD-414*. Robbie devoted considerable time and effort to research the material for his book. Since it was privately published with a limited circulation, I felt that the exploits of *Russell* warranted a larger readership. Much of the present book was drawn from Robbie's excellent narrative.

I was privileged to serve as *Russell's* Medical Officer during part of her life, and have included my recollections, but the star of this chronicle is the ship.

Russell's deck logs obtained from the National Archives served as the bones of the story; the meat was supplied by personal recollections of her crew. To place the ship's exploits in the context of the time period during which she operated, I have included material obtained from a number of internet sources.

Barry Friedman

While this book is entirely factual, I have taken an author's liberty of introducing some conversation which conveys the thoughts if not the actual words of the speaker.

Chapter 1

On a chilly, drizzly day in late November, 1938, Navy Lieutenant William Stamps Howard, Jr., hands stuffed in the pockets of his Navy blue topcoat, stood in front of a dry dock at the Newport News Shipbuilding Co. in Newport News, Virginia. Lt. Howard gazed up in awe at the ship nearing completion, still resting on a row of supporting planks and flanked on either side by scaffolds as high as the ship. From his vantage point, he could see construction workers scurrying around the vessel's deck. Welders' torches were spitting sparks. Colorful flags were strung from stem to stern, and red, white and blue bunting-covered prow, all in preparation for the ship's launching scheduled for the following week.

A small sign at the head of the dry dock read: DD414. "DD" was the Navy's designation for a destroyer.

Lieut. Howard had attended enough Navy vessel christenings to know the drill: Mrs. Charles H. Marshall, the ship's sponsor, standing on a platform at the ship's bow, would utter the traditional words, "In the name of the United States, I christen thee *Russell*. May you serve your country well. " She would smash a bottle of champagne suspended by a wide ribbon across the ship's bow, to the applause and cheers of a bevy of onlookers on the platform alongside her. The *Russell*'s horn would emit an ear-splitting blast as she slowly slipped stern first down the ways into the waters of Hampton Roads. Mrs. Marshall had named the ship to honor her late grandfather, Rear Admiral John Henry Russell, a Civil War Naval Officer.

Bill Howard, a 35-year-old, tall, slender man, had graduated from the United States Naval Academy at Annapolis in 1925. He had just arrived from Tuguila, Samoa where he had been commanding officer of *USS Ontario*, a seagoing tug. Now, although he was going from commanding a ship to a post as the second in command, his new ship was a destroyer. He was slated to be the Executive Officer of *Russell*.

Howard tingled with pride as he ogled his ship: sleek, thin-waisted and about as long as a football field. If she had been submerged in seawater, the weight of the water she displaced would be 1500 tons. Her skin was light gray at birth, later painted a camouflage-colored razzle-dazzle.

The *Russell* was the fifth of what would eventually be twelve ships of the *Sims* Class, the last destroyers built with a single engine room and smoke stack. All subsequent destroyers had two engine rooms with stacks, so if one engine was disabled, the ship would run on the second.

Survivor

Another feature was a gun that automatically calculated range and elevation for the guns, taking into account wind direction, air temperature, and ballistic factors for the guns. The director control tower for the main battery was placed high on the superstructure, for an unobstructed view. In battle, the system helped *Russell* gunners shoot down eight enemy planes and sink a Japanese destroyer.

While *Russell* was under construction in Newport News, a few miles away in Washington, D.C., Rear Admiral Alexander H. Van Keuren, Chief of the Navy's Bureau of Construction and Repair received some disturbing news. The *US Hammann,* another *Sims* Class destroyer had made a tight figure-eight maneuver at sea and, because of her top-heaviness rolled an estimated 56 degrees lasting four frightening minutes until the ship managed to right itself. The incident could have been disastrous.

Admiral Van Keuren held an emergency meeting with his staff of Naval Architects and ordered an investigation and recommendations. The group went over the blueprints of the *Hammann,* did some calculations and came up with the cause of the violent roll: The ship, as did all of the *Sims* class destroyers built to date was equipped with five 5" guns and turrets, and three quadruple torpedo mounts. The superstructure was just too heavy. Structural changes had to be made. Construction of *Russell* was put on hold while the architects went back to their drawing boards and slide rules. When they had finished, their recommendations were sent to the *Russell* shipbuilder.

Barry Friedman

To lower the ship's center of gravity, the fifth 5" gun and its turret had to be removed as did the third quadruple torpedo tube. In addition, steel plates on the bridge had to be replaced by ¼" aluminum. Finally, tons of lead sheets had to be placed in the bilges under the boilers.

Walt Singleterry, who at the time was an electricians mate aboard the *Russell* recalls "I know it was a hell of a lot of lead, I helped lug it."

When *USS Russell* was launched on December 8, 1938, almost three years to the day before the United States entered World War II., she would fight with four 5" guns. Also, on each side of the ship's main deck were four .50 cal. guns, four 20mm guns, a rack of five depth charges and four 21" torpedoes.

A year later, on 3 November, 1939, *Russell* was officially commissioned and ready for sea.

Lieutenant Commander J.C. Pollock, USN, her first skipper, had under his command six officers, including Lt. Howard, thirteen chief petty officers and 138 other enlisted personnel; a total crew of 158 men.

Russell began her shakedown cruise in the Caribbean on 12 December, 1939. During the entire month, the ship and her crew were put through rigorous maneuvers and drills designed to duplicate situations that might occur in heavy seas or battle. Liberty port stops at Guantanamo Bay, Cuba and the Virgin Islands provided short periods of rest and recreation for the hard working crew, several of whom, misinterpreting the meaning of "recreation," were overcome by the "demon rum" for which the Caribbean was noted, and were dragged back to the ship by the Shore Patrol. For these few, "shakedown" took on a new meaning. They were awarded disciplinary action by Captain Pollock.

By the end of December, 1939, the shakedown cruise was completed and the *Russell* steamed into Savannah for repair of the minor defects turned up by the demanding sea trials. *Russell* was ready to do battle.

Chapter 2

On 1 September, 1939, the German Army marched into Poland and bombarded the free city of Danzig. Two days later, Great Britain and France declared war on Germany. World War Two had officially begun.

In New York, the 1939 World's Fair was attracting large crowds with Benny Goodman and his band playing his swing version of "A Midsummer Night's Dream." The New York Yankees and the Cincinnati Reds led their respective baseball leagues by large margins. Red Skelton was performing on radio. The New York Times Industrial average closed at 176 on 1 September. On the movie screen at New York's Roxy Theater, Basil Rathbone was starring in "The Adventures of Sherlock Holmes." The weather in both New York and San Diego was clear with temperatures between 63 and 79 degrees. The Cunard Liner *Queen Mary* was approaching New York Harbor. *Moonlight Serenade* by Glenn Miller's orchestra, Bob Hope singing *Two Sleepy People* and Kate Smith's rendition of *God Bless America* were the top tunes of the day.

Survivor

The crew of the *Russell* welcomed 1940 in a New Years Day celebration in Savannah, Georgia where the ship was undergoing modifications following its shakedown cruise. For the rest of 1940, the ship's crew was engaged in drills preparing for its response to fire, collision, man overboard, steering loss and for test firing of the 5" guns.

Whether it was these painstaking preparations or pure luck, *Russell* was able to fight in sixteen major engagements of the war and emerge relatively unscathed. A survivor in the true sense of the word.

Meanwhile, in Washington, Congress was divided between members who would support England and France in their war efforts, and a group known as isolationists who were insistent that the war was Europe's and the United States had no business interfering. One of the most notable of the isolationists was Army Air Force Colonel Charles Lindbergh who had been idolized by the world for his solo flight across the Atlantic in 1927. The hero stumbled when he went to Germany in 1938 to receive the Order of the German Eagle from Nazi Field Marshal Hermann Goering. The medal was one of the highest German decorations. Lindbergh's image was further stained in May 1941, when he led a rally of 22,000 cheering America First enthusiasts in New York City's Madison Square Garden, deriding those who worried about Hitler's aggression. "The United States," he ranted, "is not in danger from a foreign invasion unless the American people bring it on by meddling in the affairs of foreign countries...

The United States must stop the hysterical chatter of calamity and invasion." Although he eventually recanted and provided valuable assistance to the war effort, Lindbergh's credibility had suffered in the eyes of the American public.

As early as 1935, Congress passed what was known as the Neutrality Act. It imposed a general embargo on trading in arms and war materials with all parties in a war. It also declared that American citizens traveling on warring ships traveled at their own risk. The act was set to expire after six months but was renewed in each of the subsequent years through 1940.

In June, 1940, France fell to the German army. British troops which had been assisting France, were stranded at Dunkirk Harbor, France, across the English Channel and seemed about to perish or be captured. Winston Churchill rallied his people in a memorable speech to Parliament. "The British Empire and the French Republic," he said, "linked together ... will defend to the death their native soil,... we shall not flag or fail. ...we shall defend our island, whatever the cost may be.

"We shall fight on the beaches, we shall fight on the landing grounds, we shall fight in the fields and in the streets, we shall fight in the hills; we shall never surrender."

In what was called "the miracle at Dunkirk," a total of 338,226 British and French soldiers were rescued by a hastily assembled fleet

Survivor

of 850 ships and boats, many of them fishing boats and pleasure craft.

Although Soviet Russia's Stalin could have prevented Hitler's invasion of Poland, he did the opposite. He provided Germany with large quantities of war materials. Now it was up to Great Britain, the only European nation to engage the Nazis. But Britain had liquidated so many assets that it was running short of cash. To make matters worse, merchant ships in the North Atlantic, carrying supplies and arms from the U.S. to Great Britain, were hammered by German submarines, the U-boats operating in groups known as "wolf packs." Between June and November, 1940, 1.6 million tons of shipping was sunk: a loss of 225 ships with 3,375 crew members.

Well before the United States entered World War Two, the *Russell* was witness to an historic event. In September, 1940, the ship was deployed to Halifax, Nova Scotia where an agreement was reached, later known as the Lend Lease Act, allowing 50 aging U.S. destroyers to be transferred to the Royal Navy and the Royal Canadian Navy in exchange for rights to bases in the Caribbean, Bermuda and Newfoundland. The Act also provided that the President could ship weapons, food, or equipment to any country whose struggle against the Axis, (Germany, Italy and Japan), assisted U.S. defense. The Neutrality Act was effectively voided. *Russell* was now unofficially in World War Two.

For the first six months of 1941, the *Russell* operated with a number of other ships at sea, and to ports in Cuba and Puerto Rico, as part of what was still known as the Neutrality Patrol Force.

On 12 July, 1941, Captain Pollock was relieved of command by Lieut. Commander Glenn Roy Hartwig, USN. A native of Detroit, Michigan, Hartwig received an appointment to the U.S.Naval Academy at Annapolis in 1920, two years after the smoke of the first World War had cleared the air. He graduated in the class of 1924. Now, at the age of 39, he was in command of a warship destined to take part in some of the fiercest battles of a second World War.

Captain Hartwig had barely unpacked his sea bag when he received orders for the *Russell* to convoy merchant ships to Iceland.

In 1941, because of the disastrous loss of merchant ships to German submarines, convoys ranging in size from 20 to 70 merchant ships, carrying arms and provisions to Great Britain, were escorted by Naval warships, mainly destroyers. After enactment of the Lend Lease program, a method was devised whereby U.S. destroyers, including *Russell*, escorted convoys from North American ports, usually Newfoundland, to Iceland. From there, ships of the Royal Navy exchanged their westbound convoys for eastbound convoys which U.S destroyers escorted to bases in the U.S. East Coast and Newfoundland. The destroyers then picked up another eastbound convoy and escorted them to Iceland. This merry-go-round occupied the *Russell* from July to December 1941.

Survivor

Although the destroyers were equipped for anti-submarine warfare, they were not immune to U-boat attacks. On September 4, 1941, the *USS Greer* was attacked by a U-boat, but was able to escape unharmed.

Two other U.S. destroyers were not as fortunate. Six weeks after the *Greer* incident, a U-boat torpedoed the *USS Kearny* resulting in the death of 11 crewmen and injury to 22 others. Although the ship was badly damaged, she managed to remain afloat and returned to Boston for repairs. Eventually, the *Kearny* returned to duty in the Atlantic.

Two weeks after the *Kearny* torpedoing, the *USS Reuben James* was torpedoed near Iceland while escorting a convoy; her entire bow was blown off and sank immediately. The aft section floated for five minutes before going down. Some of the crew were able to scramble into lifeboats, but most floated in their life jackets. Those who were immersed in the icy waters of the North Atlantic, rapidly became hypothermic, and for most of them after ten minutes irreversible damage to their central nervous and cardiovascular systems caused their deaths. Of the 159-man crew, only 44, most of whom had been able to get into lifeboats, survived.

Destroyer commanders had been faced with a dilemma trying to determine what offensive action to take against the German submarines stalking their convoys. The United States was not officially at war. On at least two occasions a destroyer captain, concerned about provoking an incident, on making sonar contact with what he was fairly sure was a U-boat, dropped depth charges at a range designed to "shake up" the submarine and encourage it to go away. After the *Reuben* Jones sinking, President Roosevelt ordered the Naval commanders to "shoot on sight" any hostile craft attacking American ships or any ships under American escort. Congress also now allowed American merchant vessels to be armed and sail to any and all belligerent ports. The Rules of Engagement were now made clear.

Towards the end of September, 1941, the Navy received reports that a German pocket battleship, the *Von Tirpitz* was lurking close to the convoy routes threatening to turn their big guns on the merchant ships.

Orders went out to *Russell* from the Commander in Chief of Atlantic Fleet. In effect they read: "Proceed with (cruiser) *Vincennes* to Denmark Straights, locate *Von Tirpitz* and engage." The term "engage" bore no relation to matrimony. Sink her!

After a few days of unproductive search, *Vincennes* left the task force and returned to her home port. *Russell* was left to deal with the German ship alone. If the *Von Tirpitz* had been engaged, the *Russell*'s little 5-inch guns would be no match for the German ship's 15-inch cannons. Fortunately, the *Von Tirpitz* was never located and *Russell* was called off the search.

Survivor

Chapter 3

At 12:53p.m., 7 December, 1941, the *Russell* was at sea off Cosco Bay, Maine, engaged in target practice. At Pearl Harbor where the time was 7:53a.m., the first wave of Japanese carrier-based planes attacked Battleship Row, Hickam Air Force Base and Ford Island in addition to other military and civilian sites on Oahu, Hawaii.

About two hours later, the attack was announced to the stunned crew of the *Russell*. They crowded around radios hungry for any information that was released, since many of the crew who had friends aboard the ships anchored at Pearl Harbor were concerned about their safety.

The first reports stated that only one battleship, the *Oklahoma,* had been set afire by bombs. The initial communiqué also reported that about 300 military personnel had been killed. The actual damage was, of course, minimized for security purposes. In fact, five battleships, three cruisers and several destroyers had been either sunk or so severely damaged that there was little possibility that they could be salvaged. Another three battlewagons and assorted warships were also hit, but could be repaired. One-hundred seventy-seven planes on the ground were destroyed. And the final figures of military personnel casualties were approximately 2300 killed, 1300 wounded and more than 900 missing.

The following day, the crew was again glued to shipboard radios listening to President Franklin Delano Roosevelt giving his "...day of infamy" speech in which he asked Congress for a declaration of war on Japan.

Many crew members on the *Russell* grumbled because the U.S. war declaration omitted Germany. After all, weren't German submarines the ones that had fired their torpedoes at U.S. destroyers sinking one and damaging another? Wasn't the *Russell* escorting merchant ships in the Atlantic, patrolling to protect them from German U-boats? A few days later the question was resolved when Germany and Italy declared war on the U.S., and the U.S. reciprocated with its own war declaration.

Although the men on the *Russell* were itching to get into the Pacific War and avenge the Pearl Harbor attack, the ship was in need of repair work to make her battle-ready. They steamed into New York Navy Yard for the necessary work expecting to get in, get out and go on to put into action all they had been training for. Briefly, they were delayed when inexperienced welders, hastily recruited, started a fire in the radio room. Fortunately, the damage was minimal and on 17

Survivor

December, ten days after the Pearl Harbor debacle, the *Russell* put out to sea.

On the bridge, Captain Hartwig broke the seal on a dispatch he'd been handed as the ship was about to depart New York Navy Yard. After reading it, he announced to the cheering crew that the *Russell* was ordered to Norfolk where she was to join Task Force 17, consisting of the aircraft carrier *Yorktown* and four other destroyers. Their destination: the Panama Canal, and through it to the Pacific.

Chapter 4

Shortly after traversing the Canal and arriving at the Pacific Ocean, the sonar operator heard through his headphones a pinging which he had been trained to associate with contact with a metallic object. Mapping the size, shape and distance of the contact, he was sure it was a submarine and excitedly reported his finding to Captain Hartwig. "Sonar contact bearing 325. Probsub." Probsub was short-hand for "probable submarine."

Moments later, at the Captain's order, the ship's alarm emitted three blaring squawks followed by the high-pitched whistle of the boatswain's pipe and his announcement: "Now hear this! Now hear this! All hands to General Quarters!"

Suddenly, a hundred pairs of feet drummed the decks The crew slapped on helmets and donned life jackets as they scurried to their battle stations. Watertight doors and hatches were slammed shut and dogged.

On the bridge Captain Hartwig picked up the TBS ship-to-ship phone and contacted Rear Admiral Frank Jack Fletcher, the task

Survivor

force's commander on the *Yorktown.* "We have sonar Probsub contact, sir. Awaiting orders."

The admiral assured Captain Hartwig that there were no "friendlies" in the area, and asked, "What is your confidence level."

"High."

Fletcher ordered, "Proceed with a depth charge attack"

"Aye, sir."

From his perch, a high stool in front of the pilothouse window on the bridge of the *Russell,* Captain Hartwig sent the order to the engine room, "All ahead flank!" Flank speed is maximum speed; for the *Russell,* 36 knots.

Quartermaster Second Class M.W. Jones was the Captain's "talker." Wearing a globelike helmet with incorporated earphones and microphone, Jones stood alongside Captain Hartwig to relay his orders. The Captain turned to Jones. "Depth charge detail standby for an attack. Ready three Mark 7 (600-pound), two Mark 6 (300-pound)."

"Aye, sir." Speaking into his microphone, Jones relayed the Captain's order.

The Captain, peering through the pilothouse window, gave course orders to the helmsman. Just behind him in the tiny chartroom, the executive officer was plotting the course and range of the contact. Minutes later he turned to the Captain and announced that they had reached the contact area.

Barry Friedman

Captain Hartwig nodded. To his talker he said, "Depth charges away!"

From the main deck, five ashcan-like depth charges catapulted from their racks on either side of the deck, and arched over the rail to drop into the sea alongside the ship.

Moments later, just aft of the ship a series of underwater explosions caused giant seawater bubbles to rise like boiling water in a pan.

Gunners Mates trained their 50 mm guns on the site of the explosions, ready to fire on a submarine if it surfaced.

Captain Hartwig ordered the helmsman to circle back around. The sonar operator reported, "Contact lost."

For quarter of an hour the *Russell* churned the sea in ever widening circles but the contact was never regained. Finally, Captain Hartwig, realizing that further searching would be fruitless, ordered the ship back on course to rejoin the Task Force.

The boatswain's whistle over the loudspeaker was followed by the announcement, "Secure General Quarters."

The event did accomplish one important result: if the contact was in fact a submarine, the depth charge attack kept it at bay giving the *Yorktown* time to sail out of its range.

Chapter 5

Shortly after abandoning the search for the suspected submarine, the *Russell* caught up with Task Force 17 enroute to San Diego. On the bridge, Lieutenant (jg) Charlie Hart, the Officer of the Deck (OOD), directed the helmsman as the ship, screened the carrier *Yorktown,* while its Douglas SBD-6 Dauntless scout planes zoomed off the flight deck for their routine Dusk Patrol. Once formed up, the planes would scout the projected route of the task force looking for enemy ships or surfaced submarines. The formation would be made up of four planes. In rapid succession, three took off, gained altitude and banked, circling over the carrier. As the fourth plane was catapulted, it lost power and plunged into the sea.

Hart had been watching the procedure and immediately called Captain Hartwig who was resting in his bridge cabin.

"Plane down!"

Hartwig rushed out of his cabin to stand alongside Hart on the wing of the bridge, keeping the sinking plane in sight through his binoculars. After Hart had apprized the Captain of the situation,

Hartwig said, "I relieve you, Mister Hart. Pass me the deck and the conn."

Nothing was actually "passed." The formality, traditional in the Navy, was designed to leave no doubt as to who was in charge of the ship's course and speed. The conn referred to control of the ship's rudder and engines.

Hart replied, "I stand relieved, sir."

Hartwig turned to the helmsman, "I have the deck and the conn. Right full rudder." Then, "All ahead flank!"

In the wake of the *Yorktown,* only the tail of the downed plane remained above water. Then it slowly sank. Two figures wearing orange lifejackets popped up at the spot where the plane had disappeared.

The carrier slowed as the *Russell* bore down on the downed airmen. When the destroyer came to a point about 50 yards from the men in the water, it came to a stop and a motor whaleboat was lowered from its davits. The coxswain manning the motorboat's rudder steered toward the airmen, and within minutes was alongside them. He and Pharmacist's Mate First Class R.L. Posey, the other crewman in the motorboat, pulled the two men out of the water. While the coxswain steered the boat back to the *Russell,* Posey briefly examined the men as best he could in the rolling boat. "Anything hurt?" he said.

Survivor

Both men shook their heads. "Naw," one them said. "The only thing hurts is we lost the fuckin' plane."

The two aviators were the first of almost 1300 the *Russell* would rescue by the end of the war. The fact that the two were alive and well was the best Christmas present they would ever had, albeit two days early.

The day after Christmas, the airmen, one the plane's pilot, the other the radioman, were returned to the carrier. Since the sea was too rough to transfer them by boat, they were sent across in a breeches buoy. The *Russell* pulled to within 30 yards of the *Yorktown* matching the carrier's course and speed. A boatswain's mate on the *Yorktown's* hangar deck fired a line from a lyle gun across the *Russell's* bow. On each ship, an end of the line was threaded through pulleys and secured to cleats producing a high-line connecting the two ships.

On the *Russell*, a breeches buoy consisting of a canvas seat, was clipped on to the high-line. One after another, the two airmen were helped into the breeches buoy and hauled across the open water to the *Yorktown*. When the breeches buoy was finally returned to the *Russell* it held ten gallons of ice cream, a treat for which the crew was most thankful.

On the last day of December, 1941, the *Russell* anchored in San Diego Harbor. For the crew, it meant ten days of leave and liberty.

Chapter 6

Six days after the *Russell*'s crew welcomed 1942, they stood by at anchor in San Diego Harbor while 5,000 First Division Marines under the command of Brigadier General Henry Larsen were loaded on to three Matson liners converted into troop transports. The transports along with the carrier *Yorktown,* two cruisers, a tanker, an ammunition ship, and a ship carrying sundry supplies made up a formidable task force. The group, with *Russell* and three other *Sims Class* destroyers patrolling on either side of the larger ships to form a protective screen, was bound for Pago Pago, Samoa, 4,000 miles to the southwest.

The voyage was far from uneventful for the men of the *Russell*. Two days into the journey, a F4F Wildcat crashed on take-off from the *Yorktown* and the *Russell* was charged with rescuing the downed pilot. Before the trip ended, two more *Yorktown* planes ended up in the water, and a sailor fell off the carrier flight deck. The pilots were rescued, but the sailor who had gone overboard without a lifejacket was lost.

Survivor

As the ships approached the equator, the heat and humidity became unbearable, a forerunner of what the *Russell* would experience at their destination. A Medical Officer had not yet been assigned to the ship, so Pharmacist's Mate Posey tended as best he could to the many victims of heat exhaustion and annoying rashes.

Two days before their scheduled arrival at Samoa, the task force received some worrisome news. A message from intelligence at CINCPAC, Commander in Chief of the Pacific Fleet, stated that an enemy submarine was operating in the convoy's path. The large ships: carrier, cruisers, and especially the slow-moving transports loaded with Marines presented inviting targets for any predator, elevating the already high level of alert on the destroyers that made up the protective screen. The relief felt by the entire task force was palpable when the convoy finally reached the relative safety of Tutuila Harbor in Western Samoa. There, under the watchful eyes of the screening destroyers, the Marines were unloaded along with their armament and supplies.

When the *Russell* finally entered the Samoan port, the anticipation of liberty for the tired crew was dashed by the warning that malaria-borne mosquitoes were a menace to anyone on the island. In addition, another disease carried by mosquitoes, filariasis causing grotesque swelling of the arms, legs and genitals, discouraged anyone from leaving the ship. Any disappointment was somewhat assuaged by the Captain's permission for the crew to swim in close proximity to the ship. Further, the presence of scantily-clad nurses sunbathing on the roof of the island's hospital provided entertainment for any crew member lucky enough to get his hands on a telescope or binoculars. It could have been a scene from the musical "South Pacific" based on the James Michener novel.

The *Russell*'s stay at Samoa was only five days. Shortly after their arrival, Captain Hartwig and the other Task Force 17 commanding officers were summoned to a meeting with Rear Admiral Fletcher in the *Yorktown.* "Because the Japanese are kicking our asses," Fletcher told them. "Walking into island after island without resistance, it's time we shake them up." The *Yorktown* task force was to form up with Rear Admiral William "Bull" Halsey's *Enterprise* task force to blast the Japanese bases on the Gilbert and Marshall Islands. Fletcher handed each commanding officer his assignment and told them to be ready to move out on 25 January.

Hartwig returned to the *Russell* and informed his crew that they were finally going to go on the offensive in the Pacific War. Although the Gilbert and Marshall raid would be undertaken by carrier aircraft, the *Russell* should expect retaliation by Japanese planes. The U.S. carriers would undoubtedly be the primary targets, and would depend on the *Russell* and other ships in the task force to protect them.

The question of the day was: where the hell are the Gilbert and Marshall Islands and who needs them?

Survivor

Chapter 7

Both the Gilbert and Marshall Islands are low-lying coral formations or atolls, barely above sea level. Their vegetation consists mainly of coconut palm trees. The Gilbert Islands stretch in a line across the equator in an approximate north-to-south direction, the equator serving to divide the North Gilbert Islands from those to the south. The main atoll is Tarawa, later to be the site of one of the bloodiest battles of World War Two.

In the late nineteenth century the Gilbert Islands became a British protectorate until 1941 when shortly after the Pearl Harbor attack, Japanese troops landed on Tarawa. A party of New Zealanders who had been acting as coast watchers were rounded up, and a few were shipped to a prison camp in Japan. From them it was later learned that another twenty-one had been beheaded.

The Marshall Islands are a group of atolls and islands just north of the equator. They lie 580 nautical miles northwest of the Gilbert Islands and are similar to them in topography. Before World War I, the Marshall Islands were under German control, but in 1914 they were taken over by Japan.

The main island of the Marshall group is Kwajalein. Shaped like the letter "U", it is one of the world's largest coral atolls as measured by area of enclosed water. Although Kwajalein's land area is only 4 square miles, it surrounds one of the largest lagoons in the world, measuring 522 square miles in size.

The primary strategic purpose of the Japanese since beginning of the Pacific War was the occupation of the Dutch (Netherlands) East Indies, now known as Indonesia, in order to gain the raw materials, principally rubber and oil they considered necessary to Japan's economic welfare.

By building strong naval and air bases in the Gilbert and Marshall Islands, Japan hoped to protect the Japanese homeland and the Dutch East Indies.

On 25 January 1942, *Russell* crew waved goodbye to Samoa and with the *Yorktown* and *Enterprise*, set out for the Gilbert and Marshall Islands. The *Russell* and three other destroyers were assigned to screen the *Yorktown*.

The objectives for the *Yorktown* Task Force were bases in the north Gilbert Islands and the southern Marshall Islands. The *Enterprise* Task Force continued further northward to raid Kwajalein, Wotje, and Maloelap in the Marshall Islands.

Survivor

With the destroyers forming a scouting line, the *Yorktown* approached her objectives in the pre-dawn darkness of 1 February 1942, and launched eleven Douglas TBD-1 Devastator torpedo bombers and seventeen Douglas SBD-3 Dauntless scout bombers.

The weather turned out to be as much of an enemy as the Japanese. Rain squalls and choppy seas made visibility and navigation a challenge. The Gilbert Islands attack group battled rain squalls and a fierce tropical thunderstorm. Despite the foul weather, and very poor visibility, *Yorktown's* aircraft attacked the few Japanese shore installations and shipping that could be seen in the mist. One group found and destroyed two large Japanese seaplanes and a gunboat.

The raid by *Yorktown* aircraft went on all day. Six planes failed to return from the raid: two were never seen again, two were forced to ditch in the water and although the crews reached shore, they were taken prisoner by the Japanese. Two other planes were seen crashing in the sea by aircraft returning to *Yorktown* and their approximate location was reported, but search planes and vessels were unable to find them. Some of the planes touched down on *Yorktown* with only a couple of gallons of fuel left in their tanks.

The attack by TF 17 on the Gilberts appears to have taken the Japanese completely by surprise. Apart from some belated and ineffective anti-aircraft fire, the main obstacle was the bad weather.

The *Enterprise* was not as fortunate. In the *Russell* radio shack the following message was received:

Barry Friedman

We were attacked by five twin-engine bombers. A near hit caused a serious fire in the machine gun battery on the port quarter, and resulted in one fatality and two men receiving superficial wounds. About two minutes later a Japanese plane which apparently was already damaged by fighter or AA fire tried to crash on deck. He missed the deck but his wing struck the tail of 6S5 which was so seriously damaged that it was partially stripped and then shoved overboard.

The material damage suffered by *Enterprise* as a result of enemy aircraft attacks was practically negligible. This in spite of the fact that the ship was subjected to bombing attacks which were pressed home with great determination by the enemy.

Vice Admiral Halsey, in command of the *Enterprise* air group, known for his plain talk, added the following comment in part:

"The inability of the 5" AA battery to knock down the formation of enemy twin-engine bombers during the first attack, before they reached the point of release is a matter of grave concern. It is believed the reason can be attributed in part to over-anxiety to hit on the part of the gun crews, as the rate of fire was exceptionally good. However, it was apparent that the target was not led sufficiently (a characteristic fault in all AA firing by inexperienced personnel), with the result that practically all bursts were late and behind the targets."

Survivor

The *Russell*'s contribution to the raid, in addition to acting as a screen, from her station 10 miles astern of the *Yorktown,* directed returning planes to the carrier. The anticipated counterattack by enemy aircraft never fully materialized. However, at approximately noon, the radar operator reported, "Bogie bearing 285 degrees at 16,000 yards!"

The Captain had the conn on the bridge. He asked, "IFF?"

"Negative, sir," reported the radar operator.

IFF, an abbreviation of "identification, friend or foe," is a means by which a coded radar signal is bounced off the responder of an unidentified aircraft. To start the identification procedure, the ship's radar operator switches the pulse frequency of his radar to a predetermined value. The IFF message is encrypted with a secret key. IFF transponders with the same secret key will be able to decode the IFF message. Once decoded, the IFF transponder will execute the message and send back a 3 pulse reply. The interrogator then marks the target as friendly while also storing its azimuth and range.

The ship was already at General Quarters. The Captain ordered the gun captains to stand ready.

Two minutes later, a four-engine plane broke through the clouds 3.000 yards from *Russell.* Through his binoculars the Captain could plainly see red "meatballs" on either wing. He ordered "Fire at will!"

Barry Friedman

The 5" gun turrets swiveled toward the plane and the cannon muzzles flamed accompanied by ear-splitting booms. The deck shuddered; the odor of cordite filled the air. The staccato of the 20 and50 mm guns shooting tracer bullets added to the din. Black dots of antiaircraft fire pocked the sky, but the plane did not appear to have been hit. It banked and was lost in the clouds apparently giving up its attack.

"Cease fire!"

The disappointment of the gun crews at having missed their target was dispelled a few minutes later when three fighter planes from the carrier could be seen at a distance swarming about a four-engine plane. It appeared to be the same enemy plane that had appeared in the *Russell*'s gun sights. The crew cheered when the Japanese plane suddenly blew apart, its fragmented fuselage falling into the sea.

Rear Admiral Fletcher was contemplating a temporary withdrawal to refuel his destroyers and await better flying weather when Vice Admiral Halsey ordered TF-17 to terminate the Gilbert-Marshall operation and return to Pearl Harbor.

Although the task forces had made their attacks under horrendous weather conditions, had lacked hard intelligence data, and had inflicted relatively little damage, the raid was successful in shaking up the Japanese command. The U.S. was no longer a passive target for their bullying.

Chapter 8

Following the Gilbert and Marshall Islands raid, *Russell,* with the rest of Task Force 17, headed for Pearl Harbor. Although the old-timers aboard had been there before, their arrival on 6 February, 1942 marked the first time *Russell* had been to the Hawaiian Naval base.

As the ship slowly entered the harbor, the crew lined the rails seeing for the first time the devastation brought on by the 7 December attack two months before. The battered hulks of six battleships protruding from the water, Diesel fuel from the sunken ships still bubbling up, shocked even the most hard-boiled among the crew.

Bob Meier, a seaman at the time, recalled, "Seeing the battleships lying on the bottom and oil still all over the harbor, I felt that we had lost the war."

The sight dampened what would normally be joy at arriving at a liberty port. Some of the crew who had friends on the sunken or severely damaged ships wandered around the base trying to find out if they had survived. When *Russell* and the rest of the *Yorktown* Task

Force finally left Pearl Harbor ten days later, there was little of the usual regret at being underway to sea.

For the first few days as the ships headed south, the normally calm Pacific was anything but. The Pharmacist's Mates were kept busy patching up shipmates who had been thrown about the rolling and pitching decks.

As the task force continued south toward the equator, the angry seas subsided. Two weeks after leaving Hawaii, the land mass of New Guinea came into view on the horizon.

The *Russell* was now part of the formidable two-carrier Task Force 11 headed by the *Yorktown* and the *Lexington*. The task force also included ten U.S. cruisers, an Australian cruiser and seventeen U.S. destroyers. Commanding Task Force 11 was Vice Admiral Wilson Brown whose flag was in *Lexington*. At age 60, Brown was one of the oldest Naval Officers.

Two days before Task Force 11 reached New Guinea, Australian coast watchers spotted a fleet of the Japanese transports carrying troops to the north coast of New Guinea at the towns of Lae, and Salamaua. They were to be staging posts for air attacks on Australian-held Port Moresby, and represented a threat to Australia itself a relatively short distance to the south. The mission for Task Force 11 was to conduct air attacks on the Japanese transports while they were unloading their troops at the beachheads.

Survivor

Japanese scout planes were patrolling to screen the landing zone, so the element of surprise would be lost if the carrier planes approached the transports from the sea to the north. Admiral Brown decided to take the task force around to the south of New Guinea. From there, the attack planes would cross the rugged Owen Stanley Mountain Range to where the troops were being unloaded.

Russell and the other destroyers, screening the two carriers, steamed through the Coral Sea to the Gulf of Papua on the southern side of the New Guinea mainland.

In the pre-dawn darkness of 10 March, *Russell* went to general quarters as the two carrier task forces, *Yorktown* and *Lexington* began launching their air groups.

On the wing of *Russell's* bridge, the OOD had his eyes glued to his binoculars as he watched in awe plane after plane catapult off the carriers' decks. He lost count after the first fifty. Later it was learned that more than a 100 planes had taken part in the raid. They had flown over the mountain range and caught the enemy by surprise.

All day, the bridge radio crackled with messages from the attacking aircraft: "Got the son of a bitch!" "Scratch one transport."

When the last of the attack group left the Japanese beachheads, the score was four transports sunk or on fire and beached at Lae, a seaplane tender damaged and dead in the water, a light cruiser and two destroyers damaged and stopped in the water, one transport listing heavily and another sunk off Salamaua. One American SBD was lost.

Later that day, Japanese Zero fighters arrived over the beachheads from their base on New Britain Island too late to protect their ships and shore installations.

Of the 104 aircraft launched by *Lexington* and *Yorktown*, 103 planes were back safely on board by noon. The raid on Lae and Salamaua provided many of the pilots with their first experience of action against warships and ground targets defended by anti-aircraft fire. Although the torpedo and bombing accuracy of some squadrons left a good deal to be desired, the raid gave the fliers valuable experience for later major actions at Coral Sea and Midway.

Later that afternoon, eight B-17s, known as flying fortresses, dropped bombs on the remaining ships at the beachhead.

Rear Admiral Fletcher thought there were enough remaining targets to warrant a second strike by carrier planes, but he was outvoted by Vice Admiral Brown who considered that the strike had been highly successful and that it was time to withdraw. Accordingly, Task Force 11 retired on a south-easterly course until dark, when the ships turned eastward heading for Noumea, New Caladonia a French possession and major base for U.S. military.

The day after the task force got underway, *Russell* received orders to be on the lookout for five floatplanes from the cruisers *Astoria* and *Louisville* that failed to return from dusk patrol. A brief

Survivor

search was unproductive and it was presumed that they had run out of fuel and were ditched. On the chance that the seaplane crews were still alive and perhaps were floating somewhere near Australia, Admiral Fletcher sent a request to the Royal Australian Air Force to assist in the search. After a week of fruitless hunt, the search was about to called off when an Aussie PBY Catalina seaplane spotted a group of five seaplanes pulled up on the beach of Rossel Island, a tiny speck of volcanic land southeast of New Guinea. After determining that the planes were "friendlies," the PBY landed close by and was greeted by a group of jubilant American airmen---the missing planes and their crews. Two of the planes had run out of fuel and landed in a lagoon at Rossel Island. The pilots of the three other scout planes wouldn't abandon their fallen comrade, besides, they were also low on fuel so they landed their craft to wait for rescue. They were out of radio range to call for help, but with the optimism of youth, they were sure they'd be found. Once they had been located, a seaplane from Port Moresby, New Guinea flew out to refuel the planes and they went airborne to the *USS Curtis* a seaplane service ship operating with Task Force 11. The only complaint the crew members had about the "adventure" was that they were out of cigarettes.

Meanwhile, as the task force knifed its way through the sea, *Russell* made sonar contact. In all probability a prowling submarine lay in the task force's path. Captain Hartwig ordered a depth charge attack, and after ten underwater explosions rocked the ship, oil rose to the surface. To the cheering crew, the evidence pointed to a"kill." However, their enthusiasm was not shared by Admiral Fletcher who cautiously rated it a "probable."

Three weeks after the air strike at Lae and Salamaua, *Russell* pulled into Noumea. They found the harbor jammed with ships of all descriptions, but it meant liberty for the crew and a source of supplies which were running low after six weeks at sea.

Chapter 9

Since its commissioning, the medical department of *Russell* as with all destroyers in peacetime, had been manned by Pharmacist's Mates. For the most part, they had been trained in Naval hospitals, and the Pharmacist's Mates on *Russell* had carried out their duties with skill and professionalism. They had treated a variety of conditions: sutured minor lacerations, dressed wounds, treated burns, and rashes, dispensed medication for minor illnesses, and when crew members presented with more complex conditions, the Pharmacist's Mates arranged for their transfer to ships or shore stations with medical officers. In peacetime, when casualties were mainly the result of shipboard accidents, the system worked. However, shortly after the U.S. entered the war, it was evident that all warships involved in combat required doctors because of the larger number of complex war-related wounds as well as crew members with more serious illnesses where it was impractical or impossible to transfer these patients to facilities where their conditions could be promptly treated.

In Noumea, *Russell* took on board its first Medical Officer, Lt.(jg) James Moran.

Dr. Moran inspected the medical department he had inherited. Sickbay was a closet-sized room located off the crew's mess hall. It contained an examination table and a desk, each of which could be folded into the bulkhead in order to provide room enough for stools on which to seat himself and a patient. There was a small autoclave, a cabinet for medications, ointments and wound dressings, surgical instruments, a safe for controlled drugs, splints, and bandages impregnated with plaster of Paris for immobilizing extremities. A small file cabinet held the health records of all the crew members.

During combat, where first aid outside of sickbay was necessary, Dr. Moran would carry a canvas knapsack containing dressings, antiseptics, morphine syrettes, and a few instruments such as hemostats and surgical scissors. The crew's mess tables and the wardroom table covered with sheets could be used as operating tables when a large number of casualties required treatment. The wardroom would serve as the triage area.

Sick call was held twice daily, morning and evening.

Dr. Moran had not fully unpacked his sea bag when he had his first patient. Vernon Skill, a Fire Controlman, had slipped on a ladder while climbing to the Gun Director platform. He sustained a lacerated scalp which required suturing.

Survivor

Liberty in Noumea was unsatisfying for the crew. They had looked forward to meeting the attractive French girls on the island. To their disappointment, they were turned down. The girls would date officers; they looked down on enlisted personnel.

It was without much regret that two days after arriving at Noumea, *Russell* was underway to join Task Force 17, commanded by Rear Admiral Frank Fletcher in the carrier *Yorktown.*

From Admiral Fletcher, Captain Hartwig learned that Intelligence had discovered a huge Japanese Fleet in the Indian Ocean. The enemy ships consisted of three battleships, five aircraft carriers, several cruisers and destroyers. They appeared to be headed toward the Dutch East Indies, later known as Indonesia, where they would support troops landing on four places along the northern coast of Java.

If the Allied Commanders were reluctant to engage the Japanese force it may have been that just about a month before in the Battle of the Java Sea, Allied casualties were heavy. The Japanese armament, especially the torpedoes outmatched those of the Allied ships. Admiral Doorman was lost along with both of the Dutch cruisers and almost all of their crews. The British cruiser *Exeter* was badly damaged by shell-fire, and was sunk along with its escorting destroyer *Encounter* two days later. Among the other destroyers engaged, *Kortenaer*, *Jupiter* and *Electra* were all sunk, with considerable loss of life. The Japanese invasion fleet was delayed, but not prevented from making a landing on Java. The surviving cruis-

Barry Friedman

ers, *Houston* and Australian *Perth*, were sunk as they attempted to withdraw to Ceylon.

By contrast, the Japanese suffered light damage to one destroyer and one cruiser, and heavy damage to only one destroyer.

But there was good news, too. On 18 April, the ship's radio carried President Roosevelt's announcement that sixteen B-25s launched from "Shangri-La (actually the *Hornet)* in a surprise raid had bombed Tokyo, Kobe, Nagoya and Yokuska. The psychological effect of the raid was greater than the amount of damage the raid produced. It served as a morale booster to Americans, and produced anxiety to the Japanese who knew only of their military successes and considered their homeland impregnable to attack.

After the war, the fate of the airmen who took part in the raid became known. All but one of the planes made a forced or crash landing. The single plane that reached a safe destination landed in Russia where the crew of five was interned. Of the other seventy-five Americans, three died when their planes crashed, sixty-four found their way to Chinese Army facilities and returned to American forces, eight became prisoners of the Japanese. Of the eight imprisoned, three were executed and one died of unknown cause while in prison camp.

At the time, the *Russell* with Task Force 11 was en route to Noumea. The crew was elated knowing that positive action against the enemy had finally taken place.

Chapter 10

Shortly after the war began, Japan's Naval General Staff advocated the occupation of Tulagi in the southeastern Solomon Islands and Port Moresby in New Guinea, which would put northern Australia within range of Japanese land-based aircraft

Unknown to the Japanese, the U.S. Communication Security Section of the Office of Naval Communications, had for several years enjoyed some success with penetrating Japanese communication ciphers and codes. By March 1942, the U.S. was able to decipher up to 15% of the Japanese code. By the end of April the Americans were reading up to 85% of the code.

In March 1942, the U.S. intercepted messages directing the Japanese carriers *Shōkaku* and *Zuikaku*a and other large warships to proceed to the main Japanese base at Truk. U.S. Intelligence concluded that from Truk they would invade Port Moresby, New Guinea, an assessment that proved correct.

On 29 April, Admiral Chester Nimitz issued orders that sent Task Force 17 consisting of the carrier *Yorktown*, escorted by three cruisers and four destroyers, including the *Russell*, towards the Coral Sea.

At about the same time, the Japanese intercepted U.S.radio traffic that led to the assumption that all but one of the U.S. Navy's carriers were in the central Pacific. The Japanese did not know the location of the remaining carrier, but did not expect an American carrier response until the operation was well underway

On 4 May, the Japanese Port Moresby Invasion Force, left Raboul in Western New Guinea. The invasion force included 11 transport ships carrying about 5,500 soldiers and was escorted by one light cruiser and six destroyers. The ships planned to pass around the southern tip of New Guinea to arrive at Port Moresby by 10 May. The Allied garrison at Port Moresby numbered around 5,333 men, but only half of these were infantry and all were badly equipped and under trained.

Anticipating the Port Moresby invasion, Rear Admiral Fletcher's Task Force 17 united with Task Force 11, commanded by Rear Admiral and consisting of the carrier *Lexington* with two cruisers and five destroyers,

Early on 3 May, the Japanese arrived off Tulagi in the southern Solomon Islands and began disembarking the naval troops to occupy the island. Tulagi was undefended. The Japanese forces immediately began construction of a seaplane and communications base.

Survivor

The same day, Admiral Fletcher was notified that the Japanese Tulagi invasion force had been sighted.

On 4 May, 60 aircraft from *Yorktown* launched strikes against the Japanese forces off Tulagi sinking a destroyer and three mine-sweepers, damaging four other ships, and destroying four seaplanes supporting the landings. The Americans lost one dive bomber and two fighters in the strikes, but all of the aircrews were eventually rescued. In spite of the damage suffered in the carrier strikes, the Japanese continued construction of the seaplane base and two days later began flying reconnaissance missions from Tulagi.

After the *Yorktown's* planes returned from their mission, *Russell* was ordered to leave the *Yorktown* screen and escort the *Neosho*, an oiler which had been brought along to refuel the ships of Task Force 17. At night, while the two ships were zigzagging, a maneuver designed to make a poorer target for submarines, *Russell's* engines suddenly became quiet. Crewmen, to whom the throb of the ship's engines was as normal as their heart beats, were awakened by the silence. Something was catastrophically wrong. The engine room "snipes" frantic to find the cause, soon determined that a pump which should have been feeding fuel to the engines had stopped. To the credit of the engine room gang, they managed to get the fuel line pump going, but they kept fingers crossed, not being sure for how long it would keep working.

Because the faulty pump made *Russell* an unreliable escort for the indispensable *Neosho,* Admiral Fletcher decided to relieve her and assigned the *Sims* to take her place. *Russell* was ordered to return to the Task Force 17 screen. It proved to be fateful decision.

On 7 May, Japanese carrier planes searching for American carriers, sighted the *Neosho* and destroyer *Sims,* and mistakenly identified them as carriers. Thirty-six dive bombers attacked the two American ships. The *Sims* was hit by three bombs, broke in half, and sank immediately, killing all but 14 of her 192-man crew. *Neosho* was hit by seven bombs. Heavily damaged and without power, *Neosho* was left drifting and slowly sinking. Before losing power, *Neosho* was able to notify Fletcher by radio that she was under attack and in trouble, but garbled any further details as to just who or what was attacking her and gave wrong coordinates for its position.

It was *Sims'* misfortune and *Russell's* luck that fate's fickle fingers had fouled up *Russell's* fuel pump.

Meanwhile, *Lexington's* air group, sank the Japanese carrier *Shōhō* and heavily damaged *Zuikaku,* another carrier. Three American aircraft were lost in the attack. On his way back to *Lexington,* SBD pilot and squadron commander Robert E. Dixon radioed the most memorable message of the Battle of the Coral Sea: "Scratch one flat top!"

Having taken heavy losses in the attack, the Japanese leaders canceled the Port Moresby mission. The Japanese aircraft all jetti-

Survivor

soned their ordnance and reversed course to return to their carriers. Ten Japanese dive bombers encountered the American carriers in the darkness, and briefly confused as to their identity, circled in preparation for landing. *Russell's* anti-aircraft went into action shooting down one plane and damaging another.

But the battle was far from over. On 8 May *Russell* received a report that an enemy force was about 170 miles away. The *Lexington* and *Yorktown* launched their aircraft to strike the Japanese ships. About the same time, the Japanese carriers launched their planes to attack the Americans. Without knowing, the opposing planes crossed paths. The gunners on *Russell*, screening the *Lexington*, waited with fingers on triggers as the expected attack materialized. While anti-aircraft fire from the entire task force dotted the sky, the Japanese planes bore in. Torpedo planes struck first, two torpedoes hitting the *Lexington.* The first torpedo buckled the port aviation gasoline stowage tanks spreading deadly gasoline vapors into surrounding compartments. The second torpedo ruptured the port water main, reducing water pressure to the three forward firerooms forcing the boilers to be shut down. Amazingly, the ship could still make 24 knots with her remaining boilers.

Russell's main battery saved *Lady Lex* from further damage when they scored a direct hit obliterating one of the incoming Japanese planes before it released its torpedo.

Barry Friedman

Moments after the torpedo plane attack, 33 Japanese dive bombers circled the two carriers from about 14,000 feet. Nineteen dove at *Lexington*, while the remaining 14 targeted *Yorktown*.

Lexington's F4F Grumman Wildcats rose to protect the U.S. carriers and fought off Zero fighters escorting the dive bombers. The F4Fs were able to penetrate the enemy formation of dive bombers shooting down four. *Russell's* guns accounted for another.

But the American planes and the anti-aircraft fire from American ships—cruisers, destroyers and carriers—were not enough to suppress the relentless attack of the swarming Japanese aircraft. Dive bombers struck *Lexington* with two bomb hits causing fires which enveloped portions of the flight deck until they were contained by the carrier's efficient Damage Control team.

Yorktown too was targeted by dive bombers one of which dropped an armor-piercing bomb in the center of her flight deck and penetrated four decks before exploding. Sixty-six men were killed or seriously wounded by the explosion. Even near misses were damaging when they struck *Yorktown's* hull below the waterline.

Three Japanese dive bombers circling *Russell* dropped their bombs barely missing the maneuvering ship but the resulting explosions knocked crew members on the main deck off their feet. Undeterred, the gun crews kept pouring 5" anti-aircraft shells at the attackers. By now the air was filled with swarming planes and anti-aircraft bursts.

Survivor

Finally, the Japanese aircraft, believing that the carriers were fatally damaged, broke off the attack. But the American F4Fs would not let them off so easily. Engaging the Japanese planes as they attempted to return to their carriers, furious dog fights filled the air. By the time the aerial duel ended, the score stood seven Japanese and six U.S. aircraft downed.

While the Japanese were attacking the U.S.carriers *Yorktown's* dive bombers and torpedo squadron were reciprocating with simultaneous attack on the Japanese carrier *Shōkaku* hitting her with two 1,000 lb bombs that destroyed the forecastle and caused heavy damage to the carrier's flight and hangar decks. The U.S. torpedoes, known to be erratic, caused the *Yorktown's* torpedo planes to miss with all of their ordnance. During the attack, two U.S. dive bombers and two Japanese Zeros were shot down. At the time, a second carrier, *Zuikaku,* was about 10,000 yards away, but was hidden under a rain squall with low-hanging clouds.

Shortly after the *Yorktown* aircraft began their attack, *Lexington's* planes arrived and continued where the others left off. Two dive bombers attacked *Shōkaku,* hitting the carrier with another 1,000 lb bomb, causing further damage. Two other dive bombers dove on *Zuikaku,* but missed with their bombs. The rest of *Lexington's* dive bombers were unable to find the Japanese carriers in the rain squall with heavy cloud cover. *Lexington's* TBD torpedo planes fired 11 torpedoes, but as with the *Yorktown's* torpedo planes, missed with all. The skirmish proved deadly for three F4F Wildcats that were outnumbered and downed by 13 Zeros.

By noon on 8 May, the U.S. and Japanese strike groups were on their way back to their respective carriers. During their return, aircraft from the two adversaries passed each other in the air, resulting in more aerial dogfights from which the U.S. planes emerged the victors shooting down two Japanese dive bombers.

Aboard *Lexington*, damage control parties had put out the fires and restored her to operational condition. Both the *Yorktown* and *Lexington* were able to recover returning aircraft. However, during recovery operations, made difficult because of the damaged decks, the U.S. lost an additional five SBD dive bombers, two torpedo planes, and an F4F Wildcat.

With fire hoses all but useless due to the torpedo hit that ruptured the main water supply, damage control teams on the *Lexington* were unable to cope with the gasoline that poured out of the broken aviation fuel tanks and had spread over the flight deck. When sparks ignited gasoline fumes, three large explosions killed 25 men and restarted the fire. By now, the *Lexington* was ablaze with fires enveloping most of the ship.

On the *Russell,* the crew watched helplessly at the raging inferno. Someone on the carrier managed to run up a flag indicating "Severe internal explosion." Shortly afterward, the Captain of the *Lexington,* realizing that his ship was damaged beyond salvage, ordered

Survivor

"Abandon ship!" *Russell* maintained a protective screen while the carrier and aircraft crews went over the side in an orderly fashion, and were picked up by cruisers and destroyers of the task force. When Captain Fredrick Sherman determined that all surviving personnel were clear of the ship, in keeping with the rules of the sea, he was the last man off.

Soon after Captain Sherman left the ship, fires spread to torpedo warheads stowed in the after hangar, and detonated in a spectacular blast. The carrier burned furiously and was blanketed by thick smoke from stem to stern.

The eventful day ended dramatically when the destroyer fired five torpedoes into the burning ship scuttling her. Two hundred and sixteen of the carrier's 2,951-man crew went down with the ship, along with 36 aircraft.

Russell and the other assisting warships left immediately to rejoin *Yorktown,* and Task Force 17 retired to the southwest. Two days later, 170 of the carrier's survivors were transferred to *Russell* from the cruiser *Minneapolis.* With the *Russell* decks crowded with personnel, crew members gave up their bunks to the "visitors" and tried to make them as comfortable as possible. The doctor and Pharmacist's Mates were kept busy treating their wounds, mostly burns. Two of the survivors were severely burned, and five days later, on 15 May, after arriving at Tonga Island, they were transferred to the hospital ship *USS Solace.* The other 168 survivors were transferred to *USS Barnett,* an attack transport, and eventually landed in San Diego.

Thus ended the Battle of Coral Sea.

Both sides publicly claimed victory. In terms of ships lost, the Japanese won a tactical victory by sinking fleet carrier *Lexington,* oiler, *Neosho* and destroyer *Sims,* versus a light carrier, a destroyer, and several smaller warships sunk by the Americans. *Lexington* represented, at that time, 25% of U.S. carrier strength in the Pacific. After the war, it was learned that the Japanese public had been informed of the victory with overstatement of the American damage and understatement of their own.

In strategic terms, however, the Allies won because the seaborne invasion of was averted, lessening the threat to the supply lines between the U.S. and Australia. The Japanese were forced to abandon the operation that had initiated the Battle of Coral Sea in the first place.

Survivor

Chapter 11

By mid-May, 1942, about a month after the Battle of Coral Sea, *Russell* was docked at Pearl Harbor. The crew had earned a well-deserved period of liberty and Pearl was one of their favorite liberty ports. It was also a time for replenishing supplies and armament. Several crew members having received transfer orders to other ships and shore facilities saluted *Russell*'s ensign and bounced down the gangway for the last time. At the same time a number of men were taken aboard as new members of the *Russell* family. They arrived in time to take part in an historic event, one that changed the course of the war: the Battle of Midway.

By way of background, the Japanese Navy strategists had achieved their initial war goals much more easily than expected. They had already occupied a number of Pacific island groups from which they could strike U.S. ships.

But Japanese hunger for power had not been sated. They turned their eyes toward the American island base at Midway. They had already destroyed much of the U.S. fleet at nearby Hawaii, so they viewed Midway as a defenseless target, one that would eliminate the already decimated U.S. Pacific fleet as an important threat. Looking even farther ahead, Japanese leaders felt that the battle-weary Americans, looking for a way out would agree to a negotiated peace.

The Japanese planned a multi-pronged attack to capture Midway. First, an attack and invasion of North Pacific's Aleutian Islands would provide a diversion. Second, would be a strike on Midway by their carrier force approaching from the northwest. Next would come a battleship force that would blast the island in preparation for invading troops and neutralize Midway's defenses. Finally, the invasion forces coming in from the West and Southwest, would actually capture Midway.

Unfortunately for the Japanese, two things went wrong even before the Midway operation began. Two of their six carriers had been in the Battle of Coral Sea. One was badly damaged, and the other suffered heavy casualties to her air group. Neither would be available for Midway.

Even more importantly, U.S. cryptanalysts had broken the Japanese military and diplomatic codes and knew its enemy's plans in detail: his target, his order of battle and his schedule. The Japanese coded message referred to their target as "AF." The cryptographers were quite certain that the AF referred to was Midway Island. Fleet Admiral Chester Nimitz, to confirm that Midway was the target, ordered a plain language message to be sent stating that "the Midway distillation plant had suffered a serious casualty and that fresh water was urgently needed."

Nimitz reasoned that Japanese radio intelligence would intercept this false message and the information would then be sent from Tokyo to the Japanese High Command. American intelligence would, in turn, intercept, and determine if the water situation at Midway was referenced. The Japanese *did* pick it up and Tokyo *did* include in an intelligence report, the statement that "AF is short of water." AF was, indeed, Midway.

When the battle opened, the U.S. Pacific fleet would have three carriers waiting, plus a strong air force and reinforced ground defenses at the Midway Base.

At 0430 in the morning of 4 June 1942, from about 200 miles northwest of Midway, Japan's four carriers began launching 108 planes to attack the U.S. base there. Unknown to the Japanese, three U.S. carriers, *Enterprise, Hornet* and *Yorktown,* were steaming 200 miles to the east. The two opposing fleets sent out search planes, the Americans to locate an enemy they knew was there and the Japanese as part of their Midway operation.

A seaplane from Midway patrolling along the expected enemy course spotted the Japanese carrier striking force and their incoming planes. Radar on Midway confirmed the approaching attack.

For most of the day, sorties by U.S. and Japanese planes filled the air between their respective carriers and Midway Island. The battle resembled a boxing match with first one combatant throwing punches, then the other one.

U.S. Navy, Marine and Army bombers based on Midway headed off to attack the Japanese fleet. Midway's Marine Corps Fighting Squadron intercepted the enemy aircraft but were met by an overwhelming force of Japanese Zero fighter planes, and were able to shoot down only a few of the enemy bombers, while suffering great losses themselves.

The Japanese planes hit Midway at 0630. Twenty minutes of bombing and strafing knocked out some facilities but did not disable the airfield. Oil tanks, the seaplane hangar and other buildings were set afire or otherwise damaged.

Shortly after 0700 six Navy TBF-1s and four Army Air Force B-26s followed by Marine Corps bombers and a formation of Army B-17s, took off from Midway and attacked the three Japanese carriers. Unfortunately, their torpedoes missed their marks

About two hours later, planes from all three U.S. carriers made a series of attacks, but, like the land-based U.S. aircraft, they did no appreciable damage to the Japanese ships. To make matters even worse, most of the torpedo planes were shot down. Squadron Torpedo Eight from *Hornet* lost all of its planes and its crews totaling 40 men. One pilot, Ensign George Gay was the sole survivor, but even his plane had been shot down and sank with its radioman still aboard. Gay was eventually picked out of the water by a PBY seaplane

Survivor

But at mid-morning the U.S. aircraft finally had success. Four squadrons of SBD scout bombers, from *Enterprise* and *Yorktown*, hit three of the four Japanese carriers scoring hits and causing enough major damage to make them inoperable. Now, the U.S. had only one enemy carrier to contend with. When a Japanese scout seaplane, probably from a cruiser, spotted the U.S. ships, the surviving Japanese carrier launched its planes.

Shortly after noon, with *Russell* screening *Yorktown,* the radar operator reported, "Large flight of bogies headed this way." He gave the course and speed of the planes. Moments later *Russell*'s bridge crew saw them diving on the carrier. *Russell's* guns accounted for two enemy bombers but seven bombers and torpedo planes survived hitting *Yorktown* with three bombs and four torpedoes. The big carrier was mortally wounded.

A half-hour later, Japanese bombers attacked the *Enterprise.* Three bombs landed on the carrier starting fires and knocking out power. The ship was dead in the water, but the Damage Control team working feverishly, put out the fires and restored power so she was able to limp along at 20 knots.

The *Russell* had lowered the Captain's gig and picked up a number of men in the water. Those that had enough strength, climbed up a cargo net that had been dropped over the side. The ones too weak were tied to ropes and hauled up on deck.

Barry Friedman

There were still more than 200 men in the water. To bring them aboard the gig would have swamped it. R.B. Russell, one of the officers conceived the idea of dragging a long line astern of a motor whaleboat, then swinging the whaleboat in an arc so the men in the water could all hang on to the rope. Within ten minutes, more than 200 swimmers were brought alongside the ship and clambered up the cargo net. In all, 497 *Yorktown* crew members were rescued and brought aboard *Russell.*

By the end of the day, U.S. planes from the *Hornet* found and bombed the remaining Japanese carrier.

The abandoned *Yorktown* was still afloat although listing badly. Captain Buckmaster, who had been rescued and hauled aboard the *Hammann* thought the carrier could be towed to a port and possibly salvaged. Accordingly, a towline was attached to the *Vireo,* a seagoing tug, and for the next day the large ship was dragged along.

On the morning of June 6, Captain Buckmaster with 29 selected officers and 141 enlisted men returned aboard *Yorktown* and found conditions the same as when the ship was abandoned. *USS Vireo* had a tow line to the ship and was keeping her headed up into the seas to prevent rolling, and was towing her very slowly. The fire in the rag stowage, which had been started by the bomb hit which pierced No. 1 elevator, was still burning.

The Commanding Officer of the destroyer *Hammann* brought his ship alongside the *Yorktown,* furnished water to fight the fire,

Survivor

furnished pumps for counter-flooding starboard tanks, and electric power to operate submersible pumps for pumping in the engine rooms. The other five destroyers, formed anti-submarine and anti-aircraft screen around *Yorktown.*

At about 1536 a salvo of four torpedoes was seen to be approaching the ship on the starboard beam from beyond the line of the screen. The first torpedo hit *Hammann* approximately amidships and caused her to sink very rapidly. Two torpedoes hit *Yorktown* just below the turn of the bilge. The fourth torpedo passed just astern of the *Yorktown.*

Approximately a minute after *Hammann's* stern sank, a terrific explosion occurred, apparently from her depth charges. This explosion killed many of *Hammann's* and a few *Yorktown* personnel who were in water and caused serious injuries to personnel from both *Hammann* and *Yorktown* who were then in the water and who were later rescued.

Since all destroyers had to be employed in searching for the attacking enemy submarines, and in rescuing *Hammann* survivors and *Yorktown* personnel who were thrown overboard by the explosion, no further salvage work could be attempted at that time. Accordingly, it was decided to postpone further attempts to salvage for the time being, to remove the salvage party to destroyers,

About 0530 on the morning of June 7 the list of the *Yorktown* was noticed to be rapidly increasing and at

Barry Friedman

0701, *Yorktown* turned over on her port side and sank with all battle flags flying.

Lieut. Joseph P. Pollard was a medical officer on *Yorktown*. He recalled the activity of 4 June: The following are excerpts of his recollections as recorded in *The Historian, Bureau of Medicine and Surgery:*

"(When attack seemed inevitable) I was called to the flight deck and sick call was suspended. Everywhere there was an undercurrent of excitement. At any moment we might be attacked.

"Meanwhile, the *Hornet* had sent off her planes, the *Enterprise* sent hers off. We could see them on the horizon like a swarm of bees—then they were gone. A report came in from Midway Island that the Japs were attacking. We hoped that our planes would make their attack on the Jap carriers while their planes were over Midway. After awhile a report came in that the Enterprise group was hitting the Jap carrier force at will. Apparently, the Japs had hit Midway with everything they had and had not expected to be attacked themselves. The *Enterprise*'s attack was completed and word came over the bull horn for our pilots to man their planes.

"Everyone was wearing anti-flash clothing and steel helmets. All was quiet—too quiet. Battle Dressing Station #1, my duty station, was manned and ready (when) general quarters sounded and Jap planes were upon us. I dived down the ladder for Battle Dressing sta-

Survivor

tion #1 and I lay flat on the deck and hoped that we would not get a bomb in the crowded dressing room or anywhere for that matter.

"By this time our anti-aircraft guns were in full bloom. I had never before heard such a roar—first the 5", then the 1.1s and 20 mm's, the 50 cal, and finally the hastily set up 30 cal. machine guns along the rail. I knew then they were upon us. Then all hell broke loose. I saw a burst of fire, heard a terrific explosion and in less then ten seconds was overwhelmed by a mass of men descending from the gun mounts and flight deck into the Dressing Station. A 500-pound bomb had struck and shrapnel had wiped out nearly all of the men from anti-aircraft guns #3 and #4 and also my corpsman who stood where I usually stood. Another corpsman was injured.

"I was overwhelmed with work. Wounded were everywhere. Some men had one foot or leg off, others had both off; some were dying--some dead. Everywhere there was need for morphine, tourniquets, blankets and first aid. Battle Dressing Station #1 rapidly overflowed into the passageway and into all other available spaces. I called for stretcher bearers to get the more seriously wounded to the sick bay where they could receive plasma, etc., but the passageways had been blocked off due to the bomb hits. So we gave more morphine, covered the patients with blankets, and did the best we could. Many patients went rapidly into shock. All topside lights were out and I never realized that flashlights gave such miserably poor light.

Barry Friedman

"I went up to the flight deck. The first thing that I noticed was anti-aircraft mount #4. A pair of legs attached to the hips sat in the trainer's seat. A stub of spinal column was hanging over back-wards—there was nothing else remaining of the trainer. The steel splinter shield was full of men——or rather portions of men, many of whom were not identifiable. Blood was everywhere. I turned forward and saw great billows of smoke rising from our stack region. We were dead in the water and it suddenly dawned on me how helpless we were lying there. Then I was called aft where there were several casualties from shrapnel which came from a near miss off the fantail. There were wounded also along the catwalk along the starboard side. We arranged to have our topside casualties lowered to the sick bay on the forward bomb elevator and this was begun.

"Suddenly, there was a great burst of steam from our stack, then another, and amid cheers from all hands we got underway. Mean-while, the Admiral and his staff had gone over to the *Astoria* and it was said that we had orders to proceed to the States at the best speed we could make. We seemed to be doing all right and began getting the ship in shape. We were really beginning to have some hope that the Japs would not return, but about 1600 our radar picked up enemy planes at 40 to 60 miles coming in fast. We had just begun to gas five F4F-4 Grumman Wildcat fighters that had succeeded landing just before the previous attack. Some had only 25 gallons aboard. Never-theless, they took off post haste. We were just hitting 22 knots but they took a long run and made it off. Just as the last one left the deck I made a dive for Battle Dressing Station #1. By the time I could find an unoccupied place on the deck there was a sickening thud and rumble throughout the ship and the deck rose under me, trembled and fell away. One torpedo hit had occurred. Then another sickening thud and the good ship shuddered and rapidly listed hard to port. I knew we were completely helpless but did not want to admit it. Just then word came over the speaker, "Prepare to abandon ship." A man lying beside me with one foot shot away and a severe chest wound turned his head towards me and asked, "What does this mean for us?" and turned his head away. He knew that he would have no chance in the water.

"We listed more and more to port until it was almost impossible to stand on the slick deck. We searched frantically for life preservers for the wounded, taking some from the dead. Our stretchers had gone below to the sick bay and we had difficulty finding enough for our wounded. All who could possibly walk did so. I went up on the flight deck and walked along the starboard edge being very careful not to slip and skid the width of the ship and off the port side. Our list was about 30 degrees. The speakers were dead and when word was passed to abandon ship, it did not get to me. Several life rafts were in the water but the lines over the side were not long enough to reach the water. Lieutenant Wilson and I tied some lines together and lowered some wounded. Meanwhile the sick bay wounded was being lowered from the hanger deck. Captain Buckmaster came up and said to abandon ship. I told him I was waiting to get off all the wounded and that we had searched the topside structure and the catwalks and I was sure that we had every man that was alive from this area on the life rafts. He said something to the effect that 'the Captain should be the last to leave the ship.'"

"I chose a line and went over the side. Soon after I started down I began slipping. The fingers of both my hands were rather badly burned before I realized it. I released the line and dropped the re-mainder of the way into the water and swam through the oil to the raft.

"We took on board several wounded who were close by until the raft was overflowing and the few of us with life preservers had to get out and swim or hold on with one hand. As each wave broke over our heads the oil burned our eyes and noses like liquid fire. It was impos-sible to keep from swallowing some of it. Someone would swim alongside and say hold me up a minute please and proceed to vomit the oil and then swim on. We had nine stretcher cases and about 25 men on or hanging on to our raft.

"Meanwhile, our destroyers were weaving back and forth about 300 yards away picking up survivors. A passing motor whaleboat threw his raft a line and was towing it to the *Russell* but with too much speed and a mess attendant was pulled off. Instead of treading water, he began screaming and wearing himself out. Captain

Survivor

Buckmaster turned loose of his raft and swam to the mess attendant. They were both about gone when a man from our raft swam out and helped keep both of them afloat. We took the mess attendant aboard but the Captain preferred to swim."

Another account by C.R. Smith, a *Yorktown* survivor:

"I was picked up by the *Russell*. Rather I *picked up* the *Russell* as it slid by me in the water. I swam as hard as I could with my life saver on, trying to catch hold of a cargo net hanging over the side. I managed to catch the last square of the cargo net and was dragged backwards. I said a short prayer that I would still have enough strength to pull myself aboard.

"As I dropped off the rail on to the ship's deck, I remember a sailor smiling down on me. I will never forget his words. He said, 'Welcome aboard sailor.'"

By final tally, the U.S. had lost the *Yorktown* and the *Hamman,* 340 killed and 145 aircraft. The *Enterprise* had suffered severe damage but was salvageable.

The Japanese had lost 3,057 killed, aircraft carrier *Akagi,* aircraft carrier *Kaga,* aircraft carrier *Soryu,* aircraft Carrier *Hiryu,* heavy cruiser *Mikuma* and 228 aircraft.

The Battle of Midway turned the tide of the war.

Chapter 12

Midway left *Russell* looking like a pit bull who'd lost the fight. Rivets had been sheared off, a fuel tank was leaking, the rudder was badly pitted and corroded, and her supplies and munitions were depleted. It was time for an overhaul, but the war could not wait until her needs could be satisfied. She pulled into Pearl Harbor to be patched up with Band-Aids and bailing wire.

It had been weeks since the crew last had a mail delivery, so when bags of letters and packages were delivered to the ship while in Pearl Harbor, they eagerly grabbed them and suspended all routine work while they poured over their letters from family giving them news from, home, love letters from wives and sweethearts, and sadly, the dreaded "Dear John" letter informing the recipient that his former "darling" had met and married someone else.

During World War Two, letters to servicemen were delivered as V-mail. The process was the microfilming of specially designed letter sheets. Instead of using valuable cargo space to ship whole letters overseas, microfilmed copies were sent and then "blown up" at an

Survivor

overseas destination before being delivered to military personnel. The resulting letter was a miniature version of the original. The 37 mail bags required to carry 150,000 one-page letters could be replaced by a single mail sack. The weight of that same amount of mail was reduced dramatically from 2,575 pounds to a mere 45.

Magazines, specifically *Time* and *Life,* were reduced to "Pony Editions." These were less than half the size of the original and contained only the editorial content, the advertising was excluded.

With *Russell* in port, the crew took the opportunity of writing letters. To make sure the outgoing mail contained no confidential material, all letters were censored. The letters were piled on the wardroom table and   the officers went over each one. Forbidden, was any reference to anything that would be of value to the enemy, such as where they were, where they'd been, or what activities the ship had been engaged in. Every crew member was well acquainted with the phrase "Loose lips sink ships." If the officers censoring the mail found anything objectionable they would either cut in out or blacken it so that it was uncipherable. Letters that contained more than a sentence or two of censorable information were rejected and returned to the writer with the admonition that repeat violations would subject the writer to disciplinary action. Although diaries were also off limits, several members of the crew kept them. After all, who would see them except the writer? Officers self-censored their own mail although base censors would randomly check officers' letters.

Barry Friedman

In the mailbag received in Pearl Harbor was a letter addressed to Radioman First Class Joseph Hicks from his draft board in Des Moines, Iowa ordering him to "report for induction" in the military. Hicks had enlisted in the Navy in 1939 and had been aboard *Russell* through battles in the Atlantic, Coral Sea and Midway. With tongue in cheek he showed the letter to Chief Radioman Paul Curtis telling him he had to go to Des Moines for induction. "Ha Ha."

Seaman 3/c William R. Richards received a letter from his mother:

"Dear Billy,

"We haven't heard from you for weeks, but you're probably on some mission. I know you can't tell us where you have been, but we read the papers and know you're busy aboard ship. We pray for you and for your safety.

"We're all well. Dad is busy at the shop. The company got a contract from the government for some kind of pump. Flo is still working at a factory. They call her 'Rosie the riveter.'

"I wrote you before that a lot of things are rationed. That's OK with us because we know it helps you win the war, For the old Dodge, we got an 'A' sticker which allows us 4 gallons of gasoline a week. Dad and Flo take the bus to work so they consider the car non-essential. We can't use the car for pleasure with an A sticker. If you're caught, you have to pay a heavy fine. They say you can even go to jail for ten years but I doubt any one is that unpatriotic. God

Survivor

help you if you have to buy a new tire they're so scarce. A lot of foods are also rationed. We have a War Ration Book. When you buy anything that's rationed you have to take a stamp out of the book and give it to the storekeeper. A Red Stamp lets you buy a limited amount of meats, butter, fat, and oils, and even cheese. Each person is allowed a certain amount of points weekly with expiration dates. You use a Blue Stamp for canned, bottled, frozen fruits and vegetables, plus juices and dry beans, and processed foods like soups and ketchup. In addition to food, rationing clothing, shoes and, coffee are all rationed too.

"We've heard of some butchers who will sell you steaks or other meats even if you don't have the stamps to cover it. They charge high prices, of course and take a chance that they won't be caught. They call it 'Black Marketing.' We refuse to buy on the Black Market because it is unpatriotic.

"We have a sticker with a blue star on the window in the front room to show we have a son in the service. Louise Holliday has two blue star stickers for Chuck and Les, and also a gold star sticker in her window because her son Harvey was killed in action.

"Well, Billy I've written a lot because our letters don't seem to reach you very often. Take care of yourself. We can't wait until you come home.

"We love you.

"Mom, Dad and Flo."

Barry Friedman

The repair crews at Pearl Harbor worked around the clock and soon—too soon—*Russell,* patched up, was ready once again to meet the enemy. The hawser lines were cast off and the ship sailed back to join Task Force 17. For the next month and one-half, Russell was engaged in training exercises. With *Yorktown* gone and *Enterprise's* bombed flight deck still unfit for duty, the carriers *Russell* was assigned to screen were, at various times, *Wasp, Hornet* and *Saratoga.*

On 17 August, *Russell* took station screening *Hornet,* and headed southwest to support the troops fighting on Guadalcanal. On the last day of August, while in the screen of the *Saratoga* took a torpedo and *Russell* conducted an unsuccessful submarine hunt, the first of many in the long and costly campaign for Guadalcanal. On 6 September, one of *Hornet's* planes dropped an explosive off *Russell's* starboard quarter to detonate a torpedo. Another submarine search commenced. At 1452, she established contact and dropped six 600-pound depth charges. At 1513, she sighted an oil slick 1 mile by one-half mile, but contact was lost at 700 yards and never regained.

Chapter 13

In April 1942, the Japanese army and navy together initiated a plan to capture Port Moresby in New Guinea. Also part of the plan was a navy operation to capture Tulagi in the southern Solomons. The objective of the operation was to establish bases to cut the supply lines between Australia and the United States, to eliminate Australia as a threat to Japanese positions in the South Pacific.

Japanese naval forces successfully captured Tulagi but its invasion of Port Moresby was repulsed at the Battle of the Coral Sea. Shortly thereafter, the Japanese navy established garrisons on Guadalcanal in the southern Solomon Islands and on the other northern and central Solomon Islands. Importing Korean laborers, the Japanese began construction of an airfield

To the U.S. Pacific War planners, the presence of the enemy on the Solomon Islands was an unacceptable threat. On 7 August 1942 the First Marine Division landed on Tulagi and Guadalcanal with little opposition. Gaining ground on Guadalcanal however was another matter. The initial landings of Marines secured the airfield without

Barry Friedman

too much difficulty, but holding the airfield for the next six months was one of the most hotly contested campaigns in the entire war. Nightly counterattacks by the Japanese Army proved costly to the U.S. troops. In addition, Japanese warships—battleships and cruisers, nicknamed the "Tokyo Express"—sailed down "The Slot," between the islands every night and bombarded the Marines' positions.

Supplying air cover for the Guadalcanal landings were the planes of the *Saratoga, Hornet* and *Enterprise. Russell* was assigned to screen the carriers.

Two days after the Marines landed, a Japanese air attack was repelled by fighter planes before it got close to the American fleet. However, since further air attacks were expected, the three carriers and their escort including *Russell* withdrew southwards on the afternoon of 8 August to make it to a refueling rendezvous with oilers. As a result, this task force was too far south to retaliate after four heavy cruisers and several destroyers were sunk that night in a naval surface action, the disastrous Battle of Savo Island, in which the U.S. Navy found out the hard way the Japanese Navy was well practiced in night warfare using star shells and searchlights. The U.S. ships depended on radar which at the time was greatly limited by its short range. In addition, the Japanese ships were hidden from contact in the radar shadow of Savo Island.

In the Savo Island battle, the U.S. lost the cruisers *Quincy, Vincennes, Astoria,* and the Australians lost the cruiser *Canberra*-85.

Survivor

Another cruiser, the *USS Chicago* was hit by a torpedo which blew a 30 foot hole in her bow. Although she was knocked out of service for several months, she eventually returned to action only to be sunk later in the Pacific war.

Two U.S. destroyers, *Ralph Talbot* and *Patterson* suffered major damage but were repaired. The battle cost the lives of 1,077 men. The destroyer *USS Jarvis* was sunk with the loss of her entire crew of 233. However, this occurred a few days later and is usually considered a separate action from the Battle of Savo Island.

The Japanese, by comparison lost one cruiser sunk and three other cruisers moderately damaged.

As a sidebar to the battle, the actions of *Chicago's* Captain were questioned by an inquiry board. He was reprimanded, effectively blocking any further progress in his Naval career. Though the report was not intended to be made public, he learned of its implications and put a pistol to his head.

Russell again sortied with TF 17 on 17 August; took station screening *Hornet*; and headed southwest in the vicinity of the Santa Cruz Islands.

On 31 August a U.S. Navy destroyer reported the bubbles of Japanese torpedo wakes heading towards the *Saratoga*, but the 888-foot carrier could not turn quickly enough to evade the torpedoes. A moment later, a torpedo slammed into the underwater blister on her starboard side. The torpedo didn't kill any of her sailors, and it flooded just one fireroom, but its explosion caused multiple electrical short circuits leaving her dead in the water. The cruiser *USS Minneapolis* took *Saratoga* in tow while she launched her aircraft off to reinforce shore airfields. By early afternoon, *Saratoga's* engineroom crew had improvised repairs to her electrical system from the burned wreckage of her main control board. She was then able to achieve 10 knots.

Russell was temporarily detached from her screening position and directed to search for the submarine that had torpedoed *Saratoga*. Although Captain Hartwig had a general idea of the direction from which the torpedo was launched, hunting for the submarine was like trying to find a bowl of soup in the Pacific Ocean. After an hour the hunt was called off and the ship returned to its position in the screen.

For the next week, *Russell* continued escorting the *Hornet*

On 6 September, one of *Hornet's* planes spotted a torpedo wake headed for *Hornet* and *Russell.* The pilot dropped an explosive at the torpedo detonating it as it passed just off *Russell's* starboard quarter.

Russell immediately started a sonar search which successfully established contact. She dropped six 600-pound depth charges and shortly afterward sighted an oil slick 1 mile by one-half mile, but contact was lost at 700 yards and never regained. The official report credited *Russell* with a "probable" sinking of the submarine. One of

Survivor

the crewmen grumbled, "What do you have to do to get credited with a submarine sinking? Bring in the sub captain's hat?"

Barry Friedman

Chapter 14

Historians have the advantage of seeing events from the standpoint of retrospection. They know how things will eventually turn out. The officers and enlisted men on the *Russell* had no such advantage in 1942. They lived in a microcosm and saw the Pacific War through a keyhole.   What they saw was a contest that swung to their advantage one day and to their enemy the next. Their euphoria over the victory at Midway was replaced by disheartening over the defeat at Savo Island. This emphasis on Naval warfare is not meant to minimize the role of boots on the ground. The grunts wallowing through the swamps of Guadalcanal were just as much a vital part of the war as the swabbies on the decks of warships. But except for supporting the transports carrying troops to these remote islands, the *Russell* crew saw only what was on the water, under it and in the air above it.

In their vision Naval warfare was shifting from ship-versus-ship to plane-versus- plane. Aircraft carriers were becoming more important than battleships. And as guardians of the carrier fleet, it is

Survivor

understandable that *Russell's* men were frustrated at times to see their wards being killed off.

Russell had been on the scene when *Lexington* and *Yorktown* sank, and when *Saratoga* and *Enterprise* suffered damage severe enough to put them out of service. They knew a number of Japanese carriers had been sunk and damaged, but had no way of knowing how many Japanese carriers were still serviceable.

By early September 1942, only *Wasp* and *Hornet* were able to put planes in the air. And that was soon to change.

On Tuesday, 15 September, the carriers *Wasp* and *Hornet* and the battleship *North Carolina*—with *Russell* and nine other warships—were escorting transports carrying the 7th Marine Regiment to Guadalcanal as reinforcements. There was no contact with the Japanese during the day, with the exception of a Japanese four-engine flying boat downed by a *Wasp* Wildcat.

About 14:20, the carrier *Wasp* turned into the wind to launch eight F4F Wildcat fighters and 18 SBD Dauntless dive bombers, and to recover Wildcats and Dauntlesses that had been airborne since before noon. Suddenly, a lookout called out, "three torpedoes ... three points forward of the starboard beam!"

A spread of six was fired at *Wasp* from a submarine. The OOD ordered her rudder hard to starboard, but it was too late. Three torpedoes smashed home in quick succession. All hit in the vicinity of gasoline tanks and magazines. Two of the spread of torpedoes passed ahead of *Wasp* and a sixth torpedo passed either astern or under her and struck the *North Carolina*.

Lookouts on *Russell* saw the torpedo tracks and raced to the scene. She attacked with a full pattern of depth charges but the submarine had fled. No additional torpedo attacks occurred—the damage had already been done.

In quick succession, fiery blasts ripped through the forward part of *Wasp*. Aircraft on the flight and hangar decks were thrown about and dropped on the deck with such force that landing gears snapped. Planes suspended in the hangar overheads fell and landed upon those on the hangar deck; fires broke out almost simultaneously in the hangar and below decks. Soon, the heat of the intense gasoline fires detonated the ready ammunition at the forward anti-aircraft guns and fragments showered the forward part of the ship. Two gun mounts were blown overboard and the corpse of the gun captain was thrown onto the bridge where it landed next to Captain Forrest Sherman, the carrier's skipper.

Water mains in the forward part of the ship proved useless, since they had been broken by the force of the explosions. There was no water available to fight the fire forward; and the fires continued to set off ammunition, bombs, and gasoline. As the ship listed to starboard between 10 and 15 degrees, oil and gasoline, released from the tanks by the torpedo hit, caught fire on the water.

Survivor

At that point, some flames made the central station untenable, and communication circuits went dead. Captain Sherman consulted with his executive Officer, Commander Fred C. Dickey. The two men saw no course but to abandon ship, as all fire-fighting was proving ineffectual. The survivors would have to be disembarked quickly if unnecessary loss of life was not to be incurred.

Reluctantly, after consulting with Rear Admiral Leigh Noyes, Captain Sherman ordered "abandon ship." Everyone in sick bay was carried up to the flight deck, put in stretchers and lowered into rafts. or rubber boats. The only delays occurred when many men showed reluctance to leave until all the wounded had been taken off. The abandonment took nearly 40 minutes, and satisfied that no one was left on deck, in the galleries, or in the hangar aft, Captain Sherman swung over the lifeline on the fantail and slid into the sea. He was in the water about an hour and a half until rescued by one of the destroyers.

The "tin cans" carried out the rescue efforts with persistence and determination until the 1,946 men disembarked. The abandoned ship drifted with her crew of remaining dead. The *Lansdowne* drew the duty of destruction, and was ordered to torpedo the carrier until she was sunk. One-hundred-ninety-three men had been killed.

Several crew members were singled out for acts of heroism. One was Lieut. Cmdr Laurice Tatum, a dental officer who administered first aid to the wounded on the deck while fragments of ammunition were exploding all around him. When the order to abandon ship was given, Tatum was one of the last to leave. As he was going down a rope to the water, he was killed by a shell fragment.

Chapter 15

After a short respite in Noumea, *Russell* was again on the move escorting the *Hornet* now the sole survivor of the aircraft carrier fleet.

On the ground at Guadalcanal, troops were fighting a determined Japanese army.

Guadalcanal presented forbidding terrain of mountains and dormant volcanoes up to eight thousand feet high, and a coastline with no natural harbors. With a coast protected by miles of coral reefs, only the north central coast presented suitable invasion beaches. There the invading Japanese forces had landed in July 1942. Because it lay halfway between Australia and the U.S. installation in Hawaii, Guadalcanal had the strategic value of providing a base from which the Japanese could isolate Australia and possibly invade it. The island was cursed by its hot, humid climate and swamps serving as breeding grounds for hordes of malaria and dengue-carrying mosquitoes.

Prior to the American landing in early August, the Japanese had not tried to fortify all terrain features, but concentrated on the north plain area and prominent peaks. They had built an airfield at Lunga Point and many artillery positions in nearby hills. At 1,514 feet, Mount Austen stood as the most important objective to anyone trying to hold or take the north coast. The Japanese had amassed a force of some 8,400 men to hold the island and build airfields. Their naval superiority in the southwest Pacific theater assured them of the ability to bring more troops in as needed.

The U.S. First Marine Division landed on Guadalcanal on 7 August 1942, in spite of their lack of information about the terrain, the tide, and the weather; some of the Marines were even wielding WW1-era rifles. Two battalions of the Fifth Marine Regiment established a 2,000-yard beachhead very quickly, and the airfield subsequently fell under American control. It was named Henderson Field in honor of a carrier-based pilot who lost his life in the Battle of Midway.

The men of the 6th Naval Construction Battalion followed the Marines ashore and became the first Seabees to build under combat conditions. They immediately began the arduous task of repairing Henderson Field. This became a never-ending job, because as fast as the builders leveled the strip and put down Marston matting, the Japanese would send bombers overhead to drop high explosives on their work. Nevertheless, in the midst of battle, the Seabees were able to

Survivor

repair shell and bomb holes faster than the Japanese could make them. The Allied pilots desperately needed the use of Henderson Field, so the Seabees kept this precious airstrip in almost continuous operation. The first decorated Seabee hero of the war, Seaman 2nd Class Lawrence C. "Bucky" Meyer, USNR, was among the Seabees of the 6th battalion who worked on Henderson Field. In his off-time, he salvaged and repaired an abandoned machine gun, which, he used to shoot down a Japanese Zero fighter making a strafing run. For this exploit, he was awarded the Silver Star. It was, however, a posthumous award; 13 days after shooting down the plane, "Bucky" Myer was killed in action when the gasoline barge on which he was working was struck by Japanese naval gunfire.

Progress in enlarging the perimeter around the airfield was slow, with Japanese troops shelling the field, attempting to destroy or recapture the airfield. Japanese bomber planes from Rabaul in East New Britain province, Papua New Guinea, attacked Henderson Field as well. However, Allied engineers were able to keep the field available for aircraft to land and take off. Meanwhile, the American Marines slowly drove back the land elements of the Japanese force. Although the Marines held on to Henderson Field, they lacked adequate naval support while the Japanese controlled the sea.

In mid-September one of the major engagements of the Battle of Guadalcanal occurred at the Ridge, an area 1,500 yards from Henderson Field. The Japanese, charged in waves with grenades, rifles, and bayonets yelling "*banzai!*" and "Maline (*sic*), you die!" During the battle, the Japanese taunted the Americans with cries of "US Maline (*sic*) be dead tomorrow!", and "Eleanor eats shit." The reference was to the U.S. First Lady, Eleanor Roosevelt. The Marines were pushed to the last knoll of the Ridge where there were no further natural obstacles defending Henderson Field. If they were pushed back from the Ridge, they could well lose Henderson Field. The Marines held but they were running out of armament and aviation fuel. The superiority of Japanese airpower was demonstrated by their sinking a small convoy consisting of a destroyer, *USS Meredith* escorting a seagoing tug, *USS Vireo* towing a barge containing the sorely needed ammunition and fuel. The Japanese carrier planes were unopposed except for the failed but gallant attempt of the *Meredith's* guns.

Survivor

Chapter 16

Paul Mason, an Australian, since 1939 had managed a plantation in Bougainville, one of the Solomon Islands north of Guadalcanal. When the Japanese invaded the island group he went into hiding and became one of an elite cadre of coast watchers. They were an indispensable source of information radioing reports of Japanese activity to the Australians and U.S. at great danger to themselves.

In August 1942, Mason reported Japanese air reconnaissance over the flat land near Buin at the northern end of Bougainville. In September the natives reported that the Japanese appeared to be establishing themselves in the area. Mason observed tractors, trucks, guns and other equipment being landed in the area. Mason moved inland but continued to report aircraft movements. More Japanese ships started to anchor in the area between Buin and the Shortland Islands. Mason had difficulty identifying some of them so the next supply drop included photographs of some of the pages out of "Jane's Fighting Ships".

Some friendly natives would mingle with the Japanese and then report back info to Mason. One of his signals back to Townsville, Australia read as follows:-

"Our scouts being employed Kahili at Townsville. Aerodrome is expected to be completed in a week's time. Many hundreds of natives being forced to work on aerodrome. Stores and fuel spread hidden under tarpaulins. Two anti-aircraft guns set up in fuel and ammunition dump and one anti-aircraft gun on north-western boundary of aerodrome. Wireless station on beach in front of aerodrome, also eight new iron buildings. Priests and nuns interned in iron buildings on beach. Enemy troops in green uniforms with anchor badge on arm and on white hat. Scouts state 440 enemy troops but coolies too numerous to count. Weather too hazy to observe ships today."

The information was relayed to the U.S. Pacific Command who inferred that the Japanese were preparing to bring reinforcements to their troops on Guadalcanal. The orders went out to *Hornet* to conduct an air raid on the warships and transports at three sites in the vicinity of Bougainville. With *Russell* and other destroyers guarding the *Hornet*, the carrier's planes conducted a raid on the Japanese landing parties at Buin, Fasi and Tonolai. The raid was hampered by rain and poor visibility so that damage was limited to a few of the transports. However, it caught the attention of the Japanese and put them on notice that the Solomon Island campaign would not be easy.

Survivor

The Battle for Guadalcanal was fought on the sea as well as on the ground and in the air. *Russell* remained in the thick of the fight. During October 1942, she spent most of the time screening *Hornet* while the Task Force protected, as best they could, supply ships that shuttled between Guadalcanal and the large Naval base at Espiritu Santo, a distance of 550 nautical miles.

In mid-October 1942, battleship *South Dakota* and *Enterprise,* back from repairs of the bomb damage suffered in the Battle of the Coral Sea, joined the *Hornet* task force. In the *Russell* radio shack, Radioman Harris "Red" Austin received the message and commented to his chief, Paul Curtis, that with all those guns, they "must be expecting something big."

A few days later, his prediction came true. *Russell* screening *Hornet,* moved east of the Santa Cruz Islands to intercept the Japanese combined fleet of four carriers, four battleships, and over 50 escorts that were steaming south to reinforce Japanese land forces on Guadalcanal. The engagement that ensued was later named the Battle of Santa Cruz Islands

While aircraft from *Enterprise* and *Hornet* carried out strikes on the enemy fleet, Japanese aircraft appeared over the American ships. *Enterprise* was hidden from the sight of the Japanese pilots by a local rainsquall, so dive-bombing and torpedo planes swarmed over *Hornet.* In just in seven minutes she was hit by two suicide planes, seven bombs, and two torpedoes which knocked out her boilers, jammed her rudder and demolished her generator rooms. The big carrier lost all electrical power.

Murray ordered the cruiser *Northampton* to tow *Hornet*. Since the Japanese were attacking *Enterprise*, it allowed *Northampton* to tow at about 5 knots. *Hornet*, while under tow, came under attack again from another wave of torpedo bombers later in the day. A "Kate" scored another torpedo hit, and "abandon ship" was ordered. Captain Charles P. Mason, the last man on board, climbed over the side, and survivors were soon picked up by *Russell*

Radioman Frank Soscia on *Russell* recalling the battle wrote, "What a sight! A mass of flames (engulfed) her. We really smashed our bridge and antennae while alongside the carrier. The Admiral went over to the *Pensacola*. I was hoping we could save the carrier, but three dive bombers flew over and one bomb hit right in the center of the carrier and all hopes were glum. They could have towed the *Hornet* even after the last attack. We must have men in the Navy working for the Japs the way they let these carriers go without even trying to tow them."

On the last attack the Japanese plane strafed the *Russell's* deck killing one of the *Hornet* survivors. Chief Radioman Curtis and a gun captain received minor injuries. In addition to the *Hornet* survivor that had been killed in the strafing, two others died on the *Russell*, one from severe burns and a third presumably from a head injury suffered in the bombing.

Survivor

Robert B. Russell one of *Russell's* officers, wrote of his recollections in *Face of the Sea*, originally published in 1985 and revised in 1987. The following is an excerpt:

"The Captain sent me down to take charge of the patient transfer operation. The only suitable place to send the wounded was the wardroom, and soon it began to fill up, with the overflow going into the Officer's Staterooms. Finally, I was forced to remove some of the wounded on the open deck of the forecastle until room for them could be found below.

"At one point I went down to the wardroom to see how many more we could take and found wounded men lying all around moaning. The doctor, Lieut, (MC).John Robert Schmidt of course was extremely busy. I found Mess Attendant Alonzo Bryant, got him released from his GQ station and put him to work tending the wounded.

"I went back to the wardroom to see how things were going. There, in the middle of the wardroom was a slightly built, lightly complexioned man, who(m) I presumed had been sent over from the carrier because I had never seen him before, helping our doctor, giving orders to Bryant and several other men from the *Russell.* He had organized things with the medical supplies arranged in orderly groups on the table and with the wounded men lying in neat rows with access in between. Each man's wounds had been assessed and a plan had been established as to what was going to be done. I asked where the doctor from the *Hornet* was, they told me he had gone up to the Commodore's cabin. He said he had diagnosed his problem as a collapsed lung and that he was sorry but he was simply too weak to help.

"Back in the wardroom this small blond man was moving about from case to case telling the others what to do and how to do it. Dr. Schmidt had provided some plasma and this man was supervising administering blood plasma to several patients. Others were having tourniquets applied, wounds dressed, and fractures set with splints.

"(Later) the Captain called the division heads to the bridge and said he wanted to have recommendations from us for individuals deserving commendation. I right away said we ought to cite the small, blond man who had done such a terrific job with the wounded in the wardroom. The Captain told me to find the small blond man because he wanted to talk to him. He was no longer in the wardroom where he had been until the critically wounded had been transferred, but had not been seen since. Only the critically wounded had been transferred to the cruiser so the man had to be still on board the *Russell.* We went around among the crew of the *Russell* and the survivors looking for him. No one had any information about him. I asked the doctor from the *Hornet,* he said he had seen the man but assumed he was from the *Russell* because he (the doctor) did not recognize him as a Pharmacist's Mate from the *Hornet.* I spoke to all hands on the ship's P.A. system, explained that we wanted to find him to com-

Survivor

mend him and asked if he would identify himself. No one responded. While the remainder of *Hornet's* men were leaving us in Noumea I looked at every man. He was not among them. In the end we gave up. It's a complete mystery."

Meanwhile, Captain Hartwig offered to take *Hornet* under tow thinking that she might be salvaged. Because of the size of the carrier, Rear Admiral George Murray, the task force commander, assigned the tow to the cruiser *Northampton*. But when six enemy torpedo planes attacked *Hornet* the ship's list quickly increased, Rear Admiral Murray made the decision to sink her to prevent her falling into enemy hands. "Abandon ship" was ordered.

Although sea was rough, *Russell* maneuvered alongside the *Hornet* taking on board 571 of the carrier's crew. Captain Charles Mason was the last to leave the ship. While the transfer was underway, a Japanese bomber attacked through a barrage of anti-aircraft fire, dropping a bomb but missing both the carrier and *Russell* by about 100 feet. The heavy seas made the transfer of men from the carrier difficult. To Hartwig's credit, he refused to abandon the rescue in spite of fires raging on the carrier and the *Russell* slamming against *Hornet's* hull damaging the destroyer's bridge, smashing one of her life boats, and releasing a depth charge from its mount. The depth charge landed in the water alongside *Russell* causing anxious moments until one of the crewmen affirmed that it had been set on "safe" and wouldn't explode under the ship.

Barry Friedman

Two destroyers of the task force, *Mustin* and *Anderson,* were assigned to scuttle *Hornet,* but after they had fired nine torpedoes and over 300 rounds of 5" shells into the carrier's side, she refused to sink.

When a large Japanese surface force was detected on radar, the destroyers withdrew from to the area, leaving *Hornet* blazing throughout her whole length. Two Japanese destroyers fired four torpedoes into her. Finally, amid the roaring hiss of escaping air and boiling steel, *Hornet* slipped beneath the surface to her grave under 16,000 feet of water off the Santa Cruz Islands.

Hornet was only one year and six days old when she went down.

By late afternoon the battle was over. The last Japanese planes returned to their carriers and retired to their base in Truk. The U.S. task force left for their bases in Espiritu Santo and Noumea.

Historian Eric Hammel summed up the Battle of the Santa Cruz Islands as, "a Japanese victory."

The day after the battle, *Russell* crew and the *Hornet* survivors gathered on the destroyer's crowded deck. The flag was set at half mast. The men stood at attention with heads bowed and hats off while the three dead sailors, sewn into canvas shrouds, each with a 5" projectile between his legs to weigh him down, were brought on deck on flag draped-stretchers. Captain Hartwig said a brief prayer and each stretcher was tilted, the inboard end raised. One-by-one the deceased were committed to the deep.

Chapter 17

In November 1942, while *Russell* was undergoing repairs of her damaged hull in Noumea, New Caledonia the war continued to rage in the rest of the world.

The British army was pounding retreating German troops under General Field Marshal Erwin Rommell at El Alamein in the North African desert. Stalingrad, Russia was under siege by the German army which had conquered part of the city. United States troops went ashore at Casablanca, Morocco and Oran, Algeria as a prelude to invading Italy at Sicily. Air Force Captain Eddie Rickenbacker along with two members of his crew who had been forced down after leading the air raid on Tokyo, were rescued from a raft 600 miles from Samoa by a Navy Catalina seaplane. In Washington, President Franklin D. Roosevelt was battling members of Congress over his proposal that the non-military economy of the country should be unified and controlled by one civilian director. The agencies involved would be those dealing with production, manpower and supply. More than three hundred people were killed when fire broke out in Boston's Cocoanut Grove nightclub. Loss of life resulted from smoke inhalation, burns, and panic as the screaming and clawing mob were wedged in the narrow club entrances.

In the South Pacific, *Russell* following hasty repair of her damaged bridge and hull, was assigned to assist the crew of the merchant ship, *Edgar Allen Poe*. The ship which was crammed with ammunition and food supplies for the troops fighting on Guadalcanal had been torpedoed 70 miles from Noumea.

Given the location of the merchant ship's distress call, *Russell* sped to the scene. The ship was found abandoned and drifting. One of the crew mused "Maybe it's the *Flying Dutchman,*" referring to the legendary ghost ship that never makes port and is doomed to sail forever.

After a sonar search for the Japanese submarine from which the torpedo was launched was fruitless, *Russell* next conducted a search for survivors. Two lifeboats containing the *Edgar Allan Poe's* crew were located and taken aboard *Russell*. Nine crew members had sustained injuries in the attack, and were sent to the wardroom which had been set up as a triage area. None of the injuries turned out to be life-threatening; all were treated by Dr. Schmidt.

Captain Hartwig set out to assess the damage to the *Edgar Allan Poe*, found the ship still afloat, and put a skeleton crew aboard. When they reported that the ship was in no danger of sinking, a tow hawser was attached and *Russell* prepared to tow her to Noumea. However, an Australian minesweeper came on the scene, took over the tow while Russell screened the two ships.

Although the enlisted men in *Russell's* crew had previously been rebuffed by the attractive French girls in Noumea, they looked forward to liberty on the island if only for respite from the daily rush to General Quarters aboard ship. And, of course, bars that served beer and fine French wines.

The *Russell's* stay in Noumea was short. Naval intelligence had learned that the Japanese were sending a fleet of transports loaded with troops to reinforce those on Guadalcanal. On 11 November, 1942 *Russell* was back at sea escorting the *Enterprise* and cruisers of Task Force 17. *Enterprise* had been at Nouméa for repairs, but she was the only seaworthy carrier left in the Pacific fleet, and the new Japanese thrust at the Solomons demanded her presence. She sailed with repair crews still working on board continuing their repair work even during the forthcoming battle.

Her damage control officer Lieutenant Commander Herschel A. Smith recalls, "She made the open sea with her decks still shaking and echoing to air hammers, with welders' arcs still sparking, with a big bulge in her right side forward, one oil tank still leaking, and with her forward elevator still jammed as it had been since the bomb at Santa Cruz broke it in half."

For three days, *Russell* screened *Enterprise* while she launched and recovered her planes. Although the battle was fought by aircraft,

Russell's crew huddled around the radio shack listening to reports of *Enterprise*'s airmen. Her aviators helped to sink a Japanese battleship, 16 transports and damage eight more.

Lt. (jg) Richard Batten, a carrier torpedo plane pilot, recalls the Naval Battle for Guadalcanal.

"When we took off from our carrier we knew that we were going up to Guadalcanal, but we didn't know why we were going. We did know that we had to be ready for anything that might happen."

Something happened—and fast.

"On November 13, just as we rounded the point at Guadalcanal," says Lieut. Batten, "there sat a Jap battleship ready to start shelling the boys on the island. We went up into the clouds to spiral for position." Then followed a coordinated attack, and "three of our torpedoes hit the Jap ship. She went away limping - without shelling Guadalcanal."

Later in the day Lieut. Batten's squadron, re-fueled and reloaded, went out to make another attack on the battleship. "Three more of our fish found their mark," he says, "and as dusk fell she lay gutted and listing sharply. She was finally scuttled that night by her crew."

The next morning the airmen were out early looking for trouble and soon found it. A huge Japanese convoy, apparently bent on occupying Guadalcanal, was sighted. "The ocean seemed to be covered with ships. Just like ducks on a millpond," recalls Lieut. Batten. "We

Survivor

went in on an attack with our dive bombers, and in a few minutes the ocean was covered with wreckage and human flotsam."

The "Buzzard Brigade" did more than its share in breaking up this move on Guadalcanal. They were officially credited with one battleship, two transports, and one cruiser. "I don't know how many planes our gunners got," says Lieut. Batten. "I know mine got at least one. But after this flight was over we had still another job to do. Some of us dropped 500 pound bombs on landing operations and supply dumps along the beach."

Lieut. Batten will tell you that the torpedo plane is one of the finest that's ever been built - that the risks with it are no more than in any other type of fighting plane. And his conclusions are supported by the fact that during the three day battle at Guadalcanal when his squadron made six attacks, it did not lose a single man nor single plane.

The engagement was termed the Naval Battle for Guadalcanal. It is especially noted for the deaths of the U.S. Navy's only two admirals to be killed in action during a surface engagement in the war. Rear Adm. Daniel J. Callahan aboard the cruiser *San Francisco,* and Rear Adm. Norman Scott aboard *Atlanta* were killed November 13, 1942. Both were awarded the Medal of Honor.

The battle turned back Japan's last major attempt to dislodge Allied forces from Guadalcanal and nearby Tulagi, resulting in a strategic victory for the U.S. and its allies and deciding the ultimate outcome of the Guadalcanal campaign in their favor.

While the Battle of Midway is credited with turning the tide of the Pacific war, the Naval Battle for Guadalcanal, fought a month after the disastrous Battle of Santa Cruz Islands where the U.S. lost *Hornet* and the destroyer *Porter,* as well as suffering significant damage to the carrier *Enterprise,* the destroyer *Smith,* and the cruisers *South Dakota* and *San Juan,* the Naval Battle for Guadalcanal, clearly a victory for the Allied forces, helped to restore confidence in the ability of the Allies to eventually defeat the enemy.

Although *Russell'*s role was to screen the *Enterprise* during launch and recovery operations, her presence assured the airmen that their ships would be afloat when they returned from their missions.

Chapter 18

For the *Russell,* the year 1943 began on a high note.

On 14 January, while the ship was in port at Espiritu Santo, a Jeep pulled up at the gangway. The boatswain's whistle was followed by the announcement, "Lieutenant Commander W.H. McClain coming aboard."

A khaki-clad officer, a gold oak leaf pinned to his collar, hopped out of the Jeep followed by a sailor carrying a large seabag. The officer charged up the gangway, stopped to salute the ship's ensign then saluted the Officer of the Deck saying, "Request permission to come aboard."

The OOD returned the salute. "Permission granted."

The officer said, "Lieutenant Commander Warren H. McClain reporting for duty."

Captain Hartwig had been alerted to receive his replacement and stood at the head of the gangway, Lieut. Charlie Hart, the Executive Officer, standing alongside. Captain Hartwig greeted McClain while the other officers, lined up in order of rank, stood at attention. Along

Barry Friedman

the rail the crew, their clean white uniforms replacing their dungaree work clothes, likewise stood at attention.

Lieut. Hart saluted Hartwig who, weeks before, had received a promotion to Commander. Hart reported, "The crew is at quarters, sir."

Standing alongside Executive Officer Charlie Hart, a six-footer, McClain's head came up to Hart's shoulder. However, his height in no way diminished his movements. In contrast to Hartwig's calm demeanor, McClain was a dynamo appearing to be bursting with energy.

Hartwig and McClain walked to a cleared area on the fantail in view of the entire crew. Hartwig said, "I am ready to be relieved."

McClain pulled from his pocket a sheet of paper, his orders, from which he read,

"From: Bureau of Personnel order 70566

To: Lieut. Commander Warren Howard McClain, USN

When directed, detach from current duty and proceed to DD414 *USS Russell.* Upon arrival on board report to Commander Glen Roy Hartwig for duty as his relief."

McClain saluted Hartwig and said, "I relieve you, sir."

Hartwig returned the salute. "I stand relieved."

McClain faced the crew. "I am proud and honored to serve aboard this ship with a crew that has performed admirably and I am

Survivor

sure will continue to do so. Standing orders, regulations, and instructions will remain in effect."

He turned to the Executive Officer. "Take charge and continue with the ship's routine."

Hart saluted. "Aye, aye, sir." He turned to the Chief Quartermaster. "Set the watch!"

The Change of Command ceremony was over.

Commander Hartwig had been *Russell's* skipper since July 1941. He had skillfully guided the ship through major battles including Coral Sea, Midway, Santa Cruz Islands, and the Naval Battle of Guadalcanal. His replacement, McClain, was a 34-year-old Annapolis graduate, Class of 1928.

 Now it was time to move on.

But first, another ceremony was in order.

Shortly after the Change of Command ceremony, Rear Admiral Frank Sherman was piped aboard. While the crew stood at attention, he presented awards to crew members for their action during the Battle of Santa Cruz. Five of *Russell's* men received Certificates of Merit "for heroic action and outstanding performance of duty in the sea battle with Japanese Forces off Santa Cruz Islands on 26 October 1942."

The five were: Medical Officer Lieut. J.Robert Schmidt, (MC); Lieut. J.M.Caster; Anthony Ravielle, PHM 2/C; Ishmael Allen, S 1/C; and Dale G. Irwin, F 3/C.

Barry Friedman

Admiral Sherman then pinned to the shirt of Commander Hartwig the Navy Cross, a medal second in importance only to the Medal of Honor.

Hartwig's citation reads as follows:

The President of the United States takes pleasure in presenting the Navy Cross to Glenn Roy Hartwig, Commander, U.S. Navy, for extraordinary heroism and distinguished service in the line of his profession as Commanding Officer of the Destroyer *USS RUSSELL (DD-414)*, during the engagement with enemy Japanese forces north of the Santa Cruz Islands on 26 October 1942. After enemy bombs and torpedoes had seriously damaged the task force carrier resulting in raging fires and a dangerous list on that vessel, Commander Hartwig skillfully brought his ship alongside in a most seamanlike manner to assist in fighting fires on board with every means at his command. Although driven away by further enemy air attacks, he repeatedly returned to the side of the stricken carrier to continue rendering effective assistance. Later he maneuvered in the vicinity of the ship to evacuate and rescue survivors. His gallantry and intrepidity in action were in keeping with the highest traditions of the Naval Service.

Chapter 19

But there was still a war to be fought and Captain McClain had little time to mull over his new command. After a few days of training exercises off the coast of Espiritu Santo, he was notified that American aerial reconnaissance had spotted a Japanese buildup in the vicinity of Solomon Islands. Radio intelligence supported the theory that a Japanese move was imminent. *Russell* and her new commander put out to sea in company with the carrier *Enterprise* and the cruiser *San Diego,* headed toward the battle zone.

The following is a modified excerpt from an article by John Wuckovits in the March 2000 issue of *World War II Magazine.*

In late January 1943, Admiral Halsey assembled a formidable force headed toward the Solomons to meet any large Japanese attack on the ships threating the American attempt to land Marine reinforcements on Guadalcanal. One group of cruisers, headed by Rear

Barry Friedman

Admiral Robert "Ike" Giffen, sailed out to Guadalcanal's southwest coast. There they would rendezvous with transports loaded with Marines of the 2nd Division. Protecting the rear flank was the carrier *Enterprise* screened by *Russell* and seven other destroyers. Air cover was also supplied by *Saratoga* and two escort carriers, *Chenango* and *Suwannee.* In all, they comprised an armada, a mini-Navy.

From the start there was a problem. Giffen refused to step aboard Halsey's flagship because he detested Halsey's open-necked shirts and ruffled caps. Because of his experience in the Atlantic, Giffen focused on a possible submarine threat while downplaying the danger from the skies. His decision to keep the slower escort carriers with his faster cruisers and destroyers slowed the entire group to 18 knots, the maximum speed attainable by the escort flattops. Giffen, called the escorts his ball and chain, and simmered while his group inched across the Pacific toward the rendezvous point.

Giffen's force arrived toward its planned rendezvous 50 miles north of Rennell Island, 120 miles southeast of Guadalcanal, late in the afternoon of 29 January.

Because of his experience operating against German U-boats, Giffen stationed his six destroyers in a semicircle two miles ahead. While it was appropriate for the Atlantic, this formation left the ships open to air attack—the predominant method of Japanese assault in the Pacific. The cruisers were exposed to an attack because Giffen's destroyers steamed in front.

Survivor

During the afternoon of the 29th, radar screens aboard the ships registered unidentified aircraft approaching Giffen's task force. Fighters were launched from the two escort carriers, but Giffen had issued strict orders maintaining radio silence. As a result, the planes received no assistance in pinpointing the radar sightings from the *Chicago*.

The American aircraft returned to their carriers, having failed to spot anything. Never expecting the Japanese to mount an attack after dark, Giffen declined to send up another combat air patrol, despite the remaining daylight.

At about that same time, 32 Japanese torpedo bombers, so-called Bettys, took off from Rabaul. Although radar picked up the planes, Giffen did not change course, alert his aircraft or issue orders to his ships about what they should do in case of attack.

The Japanese descended toward their targets. One American sailor looked at the radar screen in *Wichita* and described it as a disturbed hornet's nest. When the planes drew within 14 miles of Task Force 18, the planes charged in.

One Betty dropped a torpedo at the destroyer *Waller*, and then strafed her and nearby *Wichita*. A heavy stream of anti-aircraft fire found its mark, however, and the plane crashed in a fiery ball near *Chicago*.

Barry Friedman

The brief attack ended in moments. The U.S. ships avoid all the torpedoes by zigzagging, and the Americans had downed at least one torpedo plane.

Giffen assumed the Japanese attack had ended. Still hoping to make his rendezvous, he halted the ships' zigzagging and headed on a straight course. While this may have increased his ship's speed it also made them easier targets.

The Japanese took advantage of Giffen's error. Although it was now dark, a second group of Bettys could clearly see the targets, since Japanese scout planes had dropped parachutes from which dangled yellow-white flares. As they slowly descended to the ocean on both sides of the columns, the flares illuminated Giffen's cruisers and destroyers. Brightly illuminated against the black backdrop of the Pacific Ocean and steaming in a straight course, the task force became an easy mark for the Japanese aviators, who focused on cruisers *Chicago, Wichita* and *Louisville*.

But the American anti-aircraft gunners had the new proximity Mark-32 shell fuses, which automatically exploded whenever the shell came near an aircraft. Gunners did not have to hit a bomber; they only had to shoot in its vicinity. The shells lived up to expectations. One Betty crashed astern of *Waller*.

A torpedo dropped from a Betty churned through the waters toward *Chicago* but missed her by only a few yards. A second torpedo smacked into *Louisville* but failed to explode.

Survivor

Two torpedoes found their marks in *Chicago* stopping her dead in the water. The first tore a huge gash, which quickly flooded two compartments and destroyed three shafts, so the cruiser's rudder could no longer be controlled from the bridge. The second flooded the forward engine room and knocked out the only remaining drive shaft. *Chicago* floated helplessly as Captain Ralph O. Davis and his crew frantically attempted to regain control and save the ship.

In an effort to keep Japanese aircraft from locating them, Giffen made a course change, reduced speed to lessen the ships' phosphorescent wakes and ordered that no ship should open fire unless a target was clearly identified. His orders, though appropriate, meant little, for the Japanese had already broken off their attack and were heading back to Rabaul.

Now the focus switched to saving the crippled *Chicago*. Work crews aboard the stricken cruiser restored some power from emergency diesel generators, extinguished two fires and started flooding the portside bilges to counteract the ship's 11-degree starboard list. The *Louisville* took Chicago under tow in the darkness and started towing her at 4 knots. They hoped to reach Espiritu Santo, where repairs could be made to the damaged cruiser.

They never made it. Admiral Halsey ordered the ships to head toward Efate, leaving only six destroyers to screen the *Chicago*. That meant that most of the air umbrella and anti-aircraft guns headed away from the area. To provide some air cover, Halsey moved the escort carriers *Chenango* and *Suwannee* closer and ordered a group including *Russell* and the carrier *Enterprise* to steam toward the stricken cruiser. That same afternoon, *Louisville* transferred the towline to the tug *Navajo*, which had sped to the scene.

During the afternoon of 30 January, a group of Japanese aircraft was south of New Georgia and headed toward Rennell Island. Four American fighters spotted an advance Japanese plane and chased it leaving *Chicago* with no immediate air cover.

At first it appeared the Japanese force would target *Enterprise*, 40 miles southeast of *Chicago,* but because *Enterprise* was well protected, the Japanese went after *Chicago*. As the Japanese started their run toward the cruiser, four U.S. fighters from *Enterprise* sped toward the action. They charged straight into anti-aircraft fire from their own ships chasing the Japanese aircraft and shot one down.

While a small group of planes sped to the aid of *Chicago*, the Japanese entered their final run-in. One destroyer, *La Vallette*, stood squarely between the Japanese torpedo planes and the cruiser, determined to prevent any aircraft from getting beyond her. *La Vallette* opened a furious fire when the enemy came within 10,000 yards. Her anti-aircraft batteries, combined with *Chicago*'s, brought down six Japanese planes. The Japanese, however, were able to inflict some damage of their own. A torpedo churned toward *La Vallette* and ripped into her forward engine room flooding it. The ship's damage control officer and 20 other men died in the explosion.

Survivor

Water Tender Second Class M.W. Tollberg on *La Vallette* was severely burned and blinded by a spurt of live steam from a damaged pipe. Although in enormous pain, Tollberg still managed to climb topside and reach an oil valve that needed to be closed. Later, he was found by the ship's medical officer still clutching the oil valve in a heroic attempt to close it. Tollberg died two hours later.

Although damaged, *La Vallette* eventually steamed out of the battle area under her own power. Another ship rigged a towline and slowly towed the battered destroyer toward safer waters.

The tug *Navajo* had *Chicago* under tow when lookouts spotted five torpedo wakes heading toward the cruiser. Four torpedoes tore into her starting a raging inferno below decks. The cruiser listed and started to sink.

Captain Davis in *Chicago* ordered *Navajo* to cut the towline and told his crew to abandon ship. Twenty minutes after the first torpedo exploded, the ship rolled slowly over on her starboard side and settled by the stern, with colors flying. Six officers and 56 enlisted men went down with the ship. Over 1,000 survived and were rescued by other ships.

The Japanese had registered a minor victory in sinking *Chicago*, but they had also lost 12 Bettys and the American transports were able to land their Marine replacements on Guadalcanal without interference.

Barry Friedman

Numerous errors of judgment contributed to the loss of *Chicago*. Admiral Giffen had been so obsessed with keeping his rendezvous that he left his escort carriers behind. He had also been so concerned with the threat from Japanese submarines that his ships steamed in poor formation for defense from an air attack. American fighters lacked any coordinated fighter direction and thus could not mount an effective defense when *Chicago* was threatened. One historian labeled the mismanaged affair a "tactical ineptitude of the first order."

Nimitz had already been angered, even embarrassed, by earlier American naval losses in the Solomons. The Battle of Rennell Island did not help matters. At first, he intended to include a harsh condemnation of Giffen in his official report, but he eventually watered down his remarks, stating that the loss of *Chicago* was especially regrettable because it might have been prevented. However, Nimitz ordered that word of the cruiser's sinking be withheld from the public. He also vowed in a staff meeting, "If any man lets out the loss of the *Chicago*, I'll shoot him!"

The Battle of Rennell Island was not one of the war's conclusive encounters in the Pacific. However, it occurred at a time when American forces appeared to have swung momentum in the Solomons in their favor and to have halted the Japanese advance in the South Pacific. Any setback, no matter how small, was thus seen as a threat to the success of the American war effort.

Survivor

Naval historian Samuel Eliot Morison in his *History of United States Naval Operations in World War II*, summed up the Battle of Rennell Island.

"This defeat was due not only to a combination of bad luck and bad judgment, but to Admiral Giffen's inexperience and his determination to make the rendezvous with Briscoe on time. Halsey's endorsement on Giffen's Action Report was a scathing indictment of mistakes in judgment; that of Nimitz was more tolerant."

Chapter 20

The months of February and March 1943 were mainly spent at sea screening *Enterprise* between Espiritu Santo and Guadalcanal, zigzagging to match the carrier's course and speed. The *Russell* crew soon fell into a somewhat monotonous routine: trailing the carrier while her planes were launched and recovered during daily dawn and dusk patrols; muster each morning to account for each crew member; daily calls to general quarters; and attending to the ship maintenance. They responded to numerous sonar contacts on suspected submarines, and on at least one occasion her depth charge attack resulted in a diesel oil slick, presumably from a hit on a submarine. There had been several enemy plane contacts on radar and one attack by a torpedo plane aimed at *Enterprise*. Four of the carrier's planes were launched and after a 40-mile chase, shot down the intruder.

One activity that was not routine was Captain's Mast.

Discipline in all branches of the military is necessary to keep the unit combat- ready. Aboard ship, offense and punishment of minor infractions is dealt with at Captain's Mast.

Survivor

In early February, four crew members were brought before the Captain. The first, a Seaman First Class stood rigidly at attention as Captain McClain, reading from a report, said "You're accused of inattention to duty while on watch. Do you have anything to say in your defense?"

The accused sailor shook his head. "No sir."

McClain said, "Do you understand that your act could endanger the ship and all of your shipmates?"

The young man was close to tears. He mumbled, "Yes sir."

"Your punishment is five days solitary confinement in the ship's brig on bread and water. On the third day you may have full rations."

The sailor was led away. Since the destroyer did not have a brig, he was confined to a small locker used for storage.

The next offender was a Coxswain Third Class. While at General Quarters, he had secured gun watch without proper authority. He had no defense for his action. "You are reduced in rating to Seaman First Class," said the Captain. In addition to the demotion, the sentence also would result in reduction in pay.

The third miscreant, a Fireman Third Class, had been 15 minutes late for General Quarters. He was given 10 hours of extra duty.

The last man brought before the Captain was a Seaman Third Class, the lowest enlisted man's rating. He was an eighteen-year-old who had come aboard in Espiritu Santo, his first duty since enlisting and going through boot camp.

Captain McClain pursed his lips and shook his head slowly as he read the offense. "You are accused of refusing to obey orders and cowardliness at General Quarters."

An enemy plane had descended over *Russell* while heading toward an attack on *Enterprise*. *Russell* had been screening the carrier and her anti-aircraft guns went into action. The young man had been given the duty of carrying boxes containing belts of cartridges to one of the gunner's mates who fed the cartridge belts into one of the 20mm guns. While the gunner was screaming for more ammunition the seaman froze. It was his first exposure to combat and he stood rooted by fear with his eyes closed, his hands over his ears to block out the sound of the anti-aircraft gunfire, Another crewman saw the problem, ran over, and took the cowering sailor's job.

Captain McClain said, "What do you say for yourself?"

The youth hung his head. "I was scared."

McClain said, "Son, we're all scared but each of us has a job to do and we do it. I could have you tried in a General Court Martial. But since you've never been in combat before, I'm referring you to a Summary Court-Martial. Know what that is?"

"No sir."

"Mr. Bargeloh will explain it to you."

Captain McClain turned to his Executive Officer. "Tell this sailor what the procedure is."

McClain dismissed the proceedings

Survivor

In a Summary Court-Martial, the maximum punishment that may be imposed depends upon the rank of the accused. For an enlisted accused in the pay grade of E-5 (Petty Officer Second Class) and above, the accused may be reduced one pay-grade, be restricted for a period of 60 days, and face a forfeiture of two-thirds of basic pay for one month. For an accused in the rank of E-4 (Petty Officer Third Class) and below as was the case here, the accused may be sentenced to confinement for up to 30 days, hard labor without confinement for a period of 45 days, restriction for a period of 60 days, reduction to the pay grade of E-1, the lowest rating of an enlisted person, and forfeiture of two-thirds of basic pay for one month. As a rule, only relatively minor offenses are taken to Summary Court–Martial. Although the person accused has the right to refuse and opt for a Special or General Court Martial where his case is heard before three or five officer-judges, it is to his benefit to accept the Summary Court-Martial in that this Court has no power to adjudge a punitive discharge in any case and is not considered a federal conviction, unless the accused is represented by an attorney at the Summary Court-Martial.

A few days after the Captain's Mast, Executive Officer Bargeloh acting in all capacities: as judge, prosecutor and defending officer, supervised the Summary Court Martial. The crew members who were involved in the incident were called as witnesses and the accused sailor was given the chance to explain his side of the story.

Since he had no defense for his actions except for inexperience, his punishment was confinement for 60 days, ten hours of extra duty, and loss of three-fourths of his pay for one month. Confinement was defined as being restricted to the ship. He would not be allowed to go off for liberty.

For the rest of the crew, after a long period at sea shuttling transports and supply ships between Noumea and Guadalcanal, in late March *Russell* was awarded ten days of rest and recreation in Sydney, Australia—finally a liberty port in a big city. Here R&R meant little rest and much recreation. All hands were given maximum liberty and they took maximum advantage of the goodies: girls, bars, girls, shops, girls, and, of course, girls.

By the first week in April, they were back in the war running an escort service between Espiritu Santo, Noumea, and Guadalcanal.

Although the troops on Guadalcanal were making progress in securing the island, the air attacks on shipping did not abate. On 17 April Japanese planes based in the northern Solomons at Raboul rained bombs on a convoy *Russell* was escorting. Anti-aircraft fire was successful in preventing any serious damage although one bomb landed just astern of the ship. A few days later, sonar picked up a contact most likely from a submarine. *Russell* dropped a barrage of depth charges before losing contact but the convoy was unharmed and continued to their destination at Espiritu Santo.

Survivor

The first day in May 1943 saw *Russell* back as escort to *Enterprise* enroute to Pearl Harbor. Their arrival on 8 May coincided with the surrender of the German Army in Africa. It would be another year until D-Day when the Allied Forces would engage the German Army on the beaches of Normandy in France.

Russell was now well into her third year on the battlefront, and from the engine room to the superstructure she showed the wear and tear of the hammering she'd endured. The starboard wing of the bridge was still in shambles from the smashing it had taken from the hull of *Hornet* while fighting fires and rescuing personnel. After escorting *Enterprise* to Pearl Harbor the crew was jubilant to learn they would be sailing to San Francisco and from there to nearby Mare Island Shipyard for repairs. On 17 June 1943 the *Russell* crew, cleaned and dressed in white uniforms lined the deck as the ship passed under the Golden Gate Bridge.

Chapter 21

The orders read:

1 July, 1943

From: Bureau Naval Personnel

To: Lieutenant (jg) (MC) Barry Arthur Friedman, USNR

Persuant to order 705609, you are hereby detached from your duty at Great Lakes Naval Hospital. You will proceed to Mare Island, Vallejo, California and report for duty as Medical Officer of *USS Russell (DD414)* in relief of Lieutenant (MC) J. Robert Schmidt, USNR.

By early 1943, the powers in Washington realizing they were losing the war, asked me if I would mind helping to change the course of history. I had been in the Naval Reserve since before the war, and although I was busy interning in Cleveland at the time, if the President thought my participation was important I couldn't refuse.

Survivor

On a blustery spring morning, dressed for the first time in my brand new Naval officer's uniform, I stepped off the train at Great Lakes. Illinois, and lugged my heavy suitcase across the road to the Naval Hospital where I was to be indoctrinated.

At the main gate, a Marine guard greeted me with a snappy salute which I returned just as snappily—and knocked off my hat which went soaring into the Lake Michigan wind. The first ten minutes of my active duty career was spent chasing that damned hat, spinning like a Frisbee, down the road. After retrieving it, I returned to the gatehouse where the guard was doubled over, probably from a bad meal. When he regained his composure, he directed me to the Personnel Office for assignment.

Great Lakes Naval Hospital was conveniently laid out as a series of low buildings occupying an area only slightly smaller than the state of Montana. The Personnel Office was as far as it was possible to get from the main gate, and transportation consisted of twisting footpaths and narrow roadways. My suitcase containing everything I owned was pulling my arm out of its socket as I trudged along one of the paths. I had advanced about half a mile toward my goal, when a long black Lincoln with dark-tinted windows drove up alongside me and continued slowly in the direction I was going. From the front fender, fluttered a flag with three white stars on a blue background. The car did not pull on ahead but kept pace with my labored gait. Thank God, someone was about to offer me a lift. I smiled and inquiringly pointed a hitchhiker's thumb in the air. When a back window rolled down and a finger from inside beckoned me, I hurried alongside prepared to climb aboard. Attached to the beckoning finger was a sleeve, on which was a gold stripe that seemed to extend from wrist to elbow. Attached to the sleeve was a scowling face under an officer's cap whose visor was decorated with swirls of gold. A voice from inside the car rumbled at me. "See that flag?"

I glanced at the front fender. "The blue one?"

A grunt.

"With the white stars?"

Another grunt. "Well?"

"Well what?"

"Where's your salute?"

"I'm supposed to salute that flag?"

The driver, a sailor who until now had been staring straight ahead, turned to me. "This is the Commandant, sir. You're supposed to salute his flag when it passes."

I gulped. "I didn't know that."

The commandant bellowed. "Well, you know it now."

My brief reading of Navy Regs had not prepared me for this. "Yes sir."

"Where's your goddam salute?"

I snapped two fingers to my brim in good old Boy Scout fashion. At least this time my hat stayed on.

Survivor

The Commandant flipped a disgusted hand at me and muttered, "Goddam reservists." He turned to his chauffeur. "Drive on."

For the next two weeks I fought World War Two performing physical examinations on young nurses who were entering Naval service. If that's how I was destined to give my life for my country, so be it. I had just gotten combat-hardened (no pun intended), when I received orders to less hazardous duty: I was to proceed to the west coast to become the medical officer of *USS Russell*, a destroyer.

Air transportation during the war was restricted to people whose work was vital to the war effort: Pentagon officials, high ranking officers, and members of congress (vital to the war effort?) and whoever knew someone with authority to get an airline ticket. Others took the train. I was an "others."

I arrived at Chicago's Union Terminal once again dragging my beat-up suitcase. The train trip to San Francisco would take two days. All the sleeping accommodations and parlor chairs had been taken; I was lucky enough to get a ticket that entitled me to a coach seat anywhere I could find one. At least I wouldn't have to stand all the way.

The train was packed with servicemen of all branches of the military, some returning from leave, others, like myself, enroute to their new duty station. Entering the first coach I came to, I could barely see through the thick curtain of cigarette smoke that hung in the air. After tripping over a crap game in progress on a blanket in the aisle, I found the only unoccupied seat in the car. My seat mate, one of the few non-military people, was a little old lady who could have posed for Whistler. She was not interested in conversation, and from the time we left Chicago worked frantically with a pair of knitting needles.

During that train ride, I would soon learn what was meant by the term "Our Fighting Forces." Sailors fought with soldiers, soldiers fought with coast guardsmen and Marines fought everyone. In spite of the surrounding din emanating from the battling, the song fests and the shouts of "come seven," I found the clacking of the train wheels soporific. We had barely cleared the Chicago suburbs when I fell into a deep sleep. I awoke somewhere west of Omaha. My seat partner was gone—and so was my wallet containing about sixty dollars in cash and a government paycheck I hadn't had time to cash. In my trouser pocket I still had two or three crumpled dollar bills Ma James had somehow overlooked. My stomach began growling when I realized this money would have to buy me food for the next two days.

Until the events of September 11, 2001, World War Two was the last of this country's wars that had almost universal popular support. As a result, at many of the small towns from Nebraska to California where the train stopped to take on water, local patriotic women greeted those of us in uniform with complementary doughnuts and coffee. If we didn't have enough time to get off the train, we'd lean out of the windows (this was before the days of air-conditioned trains with sealed windows) and they'd pass the food and beverage to us. I didn't go hungry, but by the time we pulled into San Francisco, my stomach sagged with the weight of the lard and dough I'd devoured.

Without money, I'd been concerned about finding my way to my ship, which I'd learned was in Vallejo Navy Yard for repairs. But when I alighted from the train, I joined the rush of more savvy travelers who headed for the line of military buses that sped us to our destinations. For many on that train, sadly, it would be a one-way trip.

A footnote: More than a year later our ship was anchored off the New Guinea coast when we received one of our infrequent mail deliveries. In it was a small package containing my wallet, its edges chewed up and mildewed. Although the cash was gone, it still contained my government paycheck as well as a note informing me that it had been found just outside Omaha by a track-walker, a railroad employee who inspects sections of tracks. My present location had somehow been traced from my name and service number on the check. I fondled that beat-up wallet with restored faith in the human race.

At Mare Island Navy Base, I had my first view of what was to be my home for almost two years.

USS Russell. Official naval designation: DD 414. Gray sheets of steel contoured into a sleek form slightly longer than a football field and about ten yards across. Home to some 250 of us, ranging from pimply-faced 18-year-old youths, to men who at 30 had become old and grizzled.

We sailed the Pacific from the barren, treeless tundra of the Aleutians in the north, to the rocky hills dotted with grazing New Zealand sheep in the south. To islands as large as continents and to sandy atolls barely above water.

At times we were the only ship for miles in any direction, at others we were surrounded by an armada that stretched to the horizon on all sides.

We rolled and bucked and yawed in swells, and watched two-story-high walls of water break over the bridge. We slid through water as calm as a pond in midsummer.

We sprawled on wardroom benches drinking gallons of coffee, smoking cartons of cigarettes, reading and re-reading dog-eared paperbacks while from a scratchy record player Jo Stafford sang that she'd be seein' us in all the old familiar places, and Helen O'Connell sang of green eyes and of tangerine.

We became accustomed to the odor of diesel fumes, to the throb of the engines, to the creaks of the bulkheads as we lay in our bunks, to the constant echoing ping of the sonar, to the crackling static of the bridge inter-ship radio, to the shrill boatswain's whistle followed by "Now hear this...," to the chattering shutters on the signalman's light.

Survivor

Some sights and sounds and odors we could never grow accustomed to: the blaring horn of the General Quarters alarm, the pounding of feet on the decks as the crew ran to their battle stations, the slamming and dogging of hatches converting the ship into watertight compartments, the ear-shattering blast of the five-inch cannons, the ack-ack of the 20- and 40 mm machine guns, the smell of cordite and the rain of ash that hung in the air after the gunfire, the rumble of exploding undersea depth charges. We watched with pounding hearts, enemy planes that screamed down at us, weaving through puffs of anti-aircraft fire until hit, they dissolved into puffs of black smoke or exploded into balls of orange flames. And at night, we watched lines of tracer bullets from our machine guns guided to their invisible overhead targets by radar, and fears suddenly turned to cheers when a sudden burst of fire in the black sky signaled a plane had been struck and its burning carcass fluttered into the water alongside us. We watched in horror the leaping flames of a close-by ship hit by a suicide plane or a torpedo and wondered if we'd be next. We plucked from the water the sodden and oil-covered, bloody and burned survivors, and treated what we could before passing them on to larger, better-equipped ships. We watched the night horizon suddenly become aglow as a distant ship exploded, and were left to wonder. Ours? Theirs?

In pre-dawn darkness we floated slowly a few hundred yards off-shore at Kiska in the Aleutians, and Tarawa in the Gilbert Is-

Barry Friedman

lands, and Kwajalein in the Marshall Islands, and New Guinea and Biak and Wadke Islands and Leyte and Lingayen Gulf in the Philippines, and Okinawa, our five-inch battery bombarding unseen targets for hours, hoping to make landing areas safe for our troops.

We crisscrossed the equator and International Date Line more times than we could count. We broiled under the tropical sun, and turned our faces into the cool breeze at night under a sky black as velvet dotted with myriads of sparkling diamonds. We leaned on the damp rail, mesmerized by beads of phosphorescent water as the bow cleaved through the night seas. In the morning, we'd find flying fish that had landed on our decks and were flopping around helplessly until we swept them through the scuppers back into the ocean.

We judged our position by the North Star and Orion and the Southern Cross. At night, the fragrant odor of wild gardenias wafted to us from the thick foliage along the beaches of Tulagi and Guadalcanal in the Solomon Islands, and our nostrils filled with the musty smell of the jungles off the shores of New Guinea. The moon was our enemy; darkness our friend.

A sometimes terrifying, sometimes boring, but never-to-be-forgotten experience.

Chapter 22

The party that piped me aboard *Russell* that day in early July 1943, consisted of electricians, riveters, welders and painters whose greeting was, "Hey. Watch them cables, buddy. Don't trip over 'em," and from a worker shouldering a load of seven-foot steel rods, "Gangway! Comin' through." The music they played was the banging of hammers, the staccato of rivet guns, and the whoosh of welders' torches. I approached a man leaning against the rail. He was giving orders, appeared to be the foreman.

"I'm the new Medical Officer."

I could tell he was overwhelmed when he responded, "So what?"

The Officer of the Deck, Lieut. (jg) Charlie Woodman, rescued me, greeting me cordially and directed me to the wardroom. "Captain McClain is away for a couple of days, but you'll meet some of the other guys including Bob Schmidt, the doc you're relieving."

In the wardroom the Executive Officer, Charlie Hart and Bob Schmidt were drinking coffee. After we'd introduced ourselves, Schmidt gave me a tour of the ship ending at sickbay which was to be my medical office. The Chief Pharmacist's Mate, Andy Anderson was away on liberty but Schmidt introduced me to Ed Mietus, a Pharmacist's Mate Third Class who was dressing a laceration in sickbay. I'd have two Pharmacist's Mates in addition to the Chief.

From a shelf, Schmidt took a canvas bag. "This is your first aid kit. It's got all the things you need for emergency treatment of wounds or burns. Grab it when you're called to General Quarters."

I glanced inside the kit. It contained medical equipment with which I was familiar. One item was a slender brown object about the size of a book. "What's this?"

"Know anything about photography?"

"I can point a camera and click. That's about it."

"This is an eight-millimeter movie camera. You're now the ship's photographer. Unless you've got casualties to take care of you'll be shooting movies during battles or air raids. "

Over the course of my service on board *Russell,* while the rest of the crew manned their battle stations fighting the war, I saw it squinting through the eyepiece of that little movie camera. I'd send the film to COMDESPAC, Commander of Destroyers in the Pacific, to be developed. They never sent any back so I have no idea what happened to it. For all I know, those rolls of celluloid may be gathering dust in the National Archives.

On the way back to the wardroom Schmidt said, "The doctor is also the Mess Officer. You'll be inspecting food supplies when they're brought aboard, mostly perishables. Also, you'll be planning menus."

"Huh?"

"Don't worry. You work with the cook, He *really* plans the menu, but he needs your approval."

Back in Officer Country, Schmidt took me to what would be my stateroom, a six-by- ten-foot space occupied mostly by a double-decker bunk, a pair of green, steel lockers, one of which would be my closet, and a small desk that could be folded up to the bulkhead. There were eight staterooms for the officers, except the Captain and Executive Officer each of whom had a separate stateroom. At the end of the passageway was the Officers' Head with two toilet compartments and sinks, and a shower.

"You'll be rooming with Dick Edson," Schmidt said. "You've got the lower bunk."

A small wall safe sat on a narrow shelf. Schmidt spun the dial and opened it revealing a dozen, airline-sized bottles of Seagram's VO.

I gazed around the stateroom. "Is this the barroom?"

Schmidt laughed. "This is medical liquor. You'll be picking up survivors of plane crashes, or sunken ships. We give each a shot to ease their pain. That's legal."

"And one for the bartender?"

He winked. "That's a no-no. Actually, you have to account for the booze and that's the only liquor on board unless some of the crew sneaks some in."

"Has that happened?"

"Once—and he ended up in the brig. They usually have a case or two of beer locked up in the anchor locker. The officer on watch doles it out to the crew when we're anchored off one of the islands and they go ashore to play baseball or touch football.

"There are also one or two drums of alcohol in the engineering compartment. I think they use it as a coolant. It's methyl alcohol and contains a purple dye." He grinned. "A couple of crew members thought they could set up a bar on the q.t. with it. They strained some through bread which took out some of the impurities, but it was still methyl alcohol. One of the Pharmacist's Mates heard through scuttlebutt found out about it before they'd drank any. He told them the stuff was poisonous but they ignored his warning until I gave them a lecture, told them they'd go blind. That scared them enough to forget about the idea."

Schmidt pointed to the beat-up suitcase I'd been lugging around from my home to the hospital where I'd interned, and to Great Lakes Naval Hospital. It sat on the deck of my stateroom-to-be. After I'd emptied it of my uniforms and other clothing, I had planned to stow it under my bunk.

Survivor

"You'll want to get rid of that," said Schmidt. "In a rough sea it'll slide around the stateroom. Get yourself a seabag, one of those large duffle bags. You'll be able to pack your belongings in it. Also get yourself a small one, a tote bag. You can use it here as a laundry bag."

Bob Schmidt left me to pack his belongings. "I've got two weeks of leave. Then I go to my next duty station, the Naval Hospital in San Diego. Good luck—or as the Navy types say 'Fair seas and a following wind.'"

Chapter 23

Three weeks after *Russell* began her overhaul at Mare Island she was again ready for sea. Her bridge and hull had been repaired, her engines were running smoothly and her crew was rejuvenated by liberty in their homeland.

Her seaworthiness was tested by runs south to San Diego and north to Bremerton, Washington. There *Russell* joined the battleship *Pennsylvania* which had been in drydock at Pearl Harbor during the December 7, 1941 attack, had suffered relatively little bomb damage and had been back in service since early January 1942.

Alongside the massive battlewagon, *Russell* looked like a child's bathtub toy as the two-ship convoy sailed out of the Strait of Juan de Fuca, the 95-mile channel separating Canada from the United States, and entered the north Pacific Ocean, a stark contrast from the relatively calm waters farther south. The bows of the two ships then turned north, destination: Aleutian Islands.

Survivor

The Aleutians are a chain of more than 300 volcanic islands stretching from Alaska to a small group of Russian islands off the Siberian coast.

The islands are stark, barren, and treeless. The vegetation consists of tundra, a coarse grass. Most days are overcast, and rain, or in winter, snow falls on most days.

On 3 June 1942, a small Japanese force occupied the islands of Attu and Kiska. Their strategic value was their ability to control Pacific Great Circle routes. The Japanese reasoned that control of the Aleutians would prevent a possible U.S. attack across the Northern Pacific to Japan mainland. Similarly, the U.S. feared that the islands would be used as bases from which to launch aerial assaults against the West Coast. In fact, in early June 1942 Japanese planes bombed Dutch Harbor, Alaska on two occasions setting fire to an oil storage tank and damaging part of a hospital.

The battle to retake the Aleutians is known as the "Forgotten Battle", being overshadowed by the Guadalcanal Campaign which was still going on.

The Japanese invaded Kiska on 6 June, and Attu on 7 June 1942. They initially met little resistance from the local Aleuts. Most of the native population of the islands had been evacuated before the invasion and were interned in camps in the Alaska Panhandle.

On 11 May 1943, the operation by the Allies to recapture Attu began with a group of scouts known as Castner's Cutthroats. The appalling weather made it very difficult to bring any force to bear against the Japanese. The Japanese defenders did not contest the landings, but dug in on high ground away from the shore. In the bloody fighting there were 3,929 U.S. casualties: 580 were killed, 1,148 were injured, 1,200 had severe cold injuries, 614 succumbed to disease, and 318 died of miscellaneous causes, largely Japanese boo-by traps and friendly fire.

Russell was to be part of the task force that would retake Kiska.

As the *Pennsylvania* and the *Russell* sailed north from the State of Washington, the weather became the enemy. The farther north they travelled, the rougher the seas became. The ships plowed through waves that were ten to fifteen feet high. Even the battleship, large as it was, pitched in the rough seas. *Russell* took a man-sized beating. White water broke over her bow, crashed into the bridge and the ship shuddered so violently it seemed she'd break apart. The helmsman struggled to keep the ship from going abeam in a trough. The few times when she did get caught between waves, she'd roll 30 degrees in one direction, then an equal amount in the other. Anything aboard that was not securely lashed down flew from one side of the ship to the other. Anyone who had to walk on deck held on to any-thing he could grab, going from one hand-hold to another.

The old seadogs who'd been through two or more enlistments handled the brutal trip with relative ease. Many had "made their bones" in the North Atlantic where rough seas were no different from

Survivor

these. The newbies spent the time when they were not on watch either prostrate in their bunks or in the head. The older men would exacerbate their misery by blowing cigar or cigarette smoke at them. Great sport! The rolling of the ship was not as bad as the pitching when the ship would climb partway up a wave, then drop down on the other side. The mantra was, "Roll, roll you son of a bitch. The more you roll the less you pitch."

These were the days before Dramamine and other motion-sickness remedies so the sailors who were seasick had to tough it out until the weather improved, or as was the usual case, they became accustomed to the motion.

Eating became a problem, not only because it took a strong stomach to handle the violent movements, but it was a challenge to keep food from slopping out of the dishes. In the crew's mess, food was spooned into compartmented trays and for the most part stayed in place. In the wardroom, while the officers ate they held on to stanchions anchored to the deck at one end and the overhead at the other end, at three- or four-foot intervals around the table. The table itself was overlaid by a fiddleboard, a thin wooden plank with holes cut out into which plates were placed. A good part of the time the meal consisted of sandwiches

If there was a good side to the horrible weather, there was little fear of a submarine attack. The undersea craft would find it impossible to visually track a ship.

Barry Friedman

By the time *Russell* reached the Aleutian Islands, thankfully the seas had calmed. Even though it was August, the temperature rarely reached 60 degrees. Windbreakers which had been stored since leaving the North Atlantic were issued. The crew found it eerie to have daylight last well into the nighttime hours.

In preparation for the Kiska landing by U.S.troops, aircraft had bombarded the island for several weeks. When an intelligence report hinted that a Japanese force of battleships and transports were headed for the Aleutians, presumably to reinforce the troops on Kiska, *Russell* accompanied *Pennsylvania* to Dutch Harbor to load up with armor-piercing shells then rushed back to cover the Allied landing. The report of Japanese warships approaching the Aleutians turned out to be false, and for 10 days prior to the planned invasion the island was bombed from sea and air.

In the early hours of D-Day, 15 August, *Russell* along with three battleships and a heavy cruiser stood off-shore raking the landing beaches with shellfire. The invasion force of 34,426 Allied troops, went ashore on the west side of the island expecting to find the Japanese waiting on the high ground. The landings were unopposed for a good reason: The island had been abandoned. Under the cover of fog, the Japanese, who decided that their position in Kiska was vulnerable, had removed their troops two weeks before without the Allies noticing.

Chapter 24

Following the Aleutian Campaign, *Russell* headed south to Pearl Harbor where wreckage from the 7 December 1941 attack was still in evidence, the water of the Harbor still iridescent from the oil seeping from the sunken ships. But when Diamondhead, the iconic landmark of Oahu came into view, the anticipation of liberty in that magical island had the crew salivating.

Honolulu had many attractions, but for servicemen during World War Two there were none more inviting than Hotel Street. With bars, tattoo parlors and a row of brothels, it became known as the street "where you can get stewed, screwed and tattooed." From morning until the nighttime curfew, long lines of enlisted soldiers, sailors and Marines stood waiting for their turn to pay "three bucks for three minutes of fucks."

As the ship's doctor I felt the responsibility of warning the crew of the peril associated with the pleasure. To the crew assembled in the enlisted men's mess hall, I described in lurid detail the painful treatment of gonorrhea, and the dementia and other neurologic disa-

bilities that could result from late stage syphilis. Treatment of gonorrhea in 1943, before the advent of penicillin, required hospitalization,
and for stricture of the urethra resulting from the inflammation,
curved metallic sounds were inserted into the penis to dilate it. I told
them how they could minimize the risk by using condoms and
prophylactics. The latter were small tubes containing an ointment of
calomel, or mercury chloride, which was squirted into the opening of
the penis. Because venereal diseases resulted from injudicious sexual
conduct and incapacitated the affected individual, those infected
were subject to punishment ranging from loss of rating and pay to
court martial.

While the younger men, really teenagers, listened to my lecture
with open-mouthed attentiveness, the older men sat back and
yawned. They quietly told the youngsters "You're not a man until
you've had the "clap," or "a dose," i.e. gonorrhea.

To insure that my words of wisdom were not ignored, when the
crew lined up for liberty, one of the Pharmacist's Mates and I stood
at the head of the gangway and passed out to each a condom and a
tube of the prophylactic.

When the last of the liberty party had thrown their salute to the
ship's ensign, I leaned on the rail feeling as Edward Jenner must
have felt when he eradicated smallpox—until I walked down the
gangway. Strewn along the dockside were the intact packets of condoms and tubes of prophylactic ointment. Either my crew had

Survivor

planned to spend their leisure time in celibacy, or I was suffering from a delusion of grandeur. A week later, when two members of the crew appeared in sickbay complaining of burning on urination, and at "short arm inspection," a primitive ceremony where the crew lines up for inspection of genitals, another case of urethral discharge was discovered, I came to the realization that steaming hormones trumped caution.

The notation in *Russell*'s log read, "27 Sept 1943. 0800 outward bound Pearl Harbor for Wellington, New Zealand."

As we cruised out the channel to the open sea, Lieut.(j.g.) Joe Powers was leaning on the foredeck rail alongside me. Powers, a ruddy-faced, roly-poly from Chicago, in real life was a recent law school graduate. Aboard ship he was communications officers, privy to all information. He said, "I understand we're making a stop at Fiji on the way."

Fiji Islands. My mind conjured up images of spear-carrying, brown, South Sea island natives, small animal bones piercing their noses.

I hurried to the wardroom and grabbed the dog-eared atlas from the book rack. The Fiji Islands lay about 3000 nautical miles south of Hawaii. My scope of geography was gradually widening.

In 1943, we thought of the Pacific Islands as belonging either to "us" or to "them." They, the Japanese, were rapidly island-hopping, establishing bases as they hopped, island to island, toward the rich mineral resources of the Netherland East Indies. The Philippines and Java were already theirs. We drew a line in the water at Guadalcanal in the Solomon Islands vowing to block any further advance. We and our allies, the Australians, fortified our resistance by establishing air bases in the New Hebrides, New Caledonia and Fiji.

Six days after leaving Pearl, having crossed both the equator and International Date Line, we docked at the Fijian capital, Suva. The harbor, bordered by a clean grassy park with palm trees, and beyond, several one-story wooden and stucco buildings, was that of a sleepy South Sea Island with no evidence that fierce fighting had raged nine hundred miles to the west in the Solomon Islands.

A dozen weathered fishing boats floated at anchor in the harbor, but ours was the only Navy vessel. The dockworkers who assisted with the mooring lines were all Indian, not a cannibal in sight.

Shortly after we docked, Powers and I went ashore. In the afternoon heat and humidity that had our khaki uniform shirts sticking to our backs, we wandered into Suva, no more than 500 yards from where we had docked, and found ourselves in a small town with shops whose windows were shielded from the equatorial sun by awnings. The few people in the streets were mostly dark-skinned East Indians. The men, some wearing turbans, were dressed in white, collarless long shirts that came down to their knees; the women wore saris. Two or three women whose fair hair peeked from under wide-

Survivor

brimmed hats, and who wore flower-patterned dresses, strolled in low-heeled shoes under parasols. They were reminders that Fiji was a British protectorate. The quiet was broken only by the clop of horse-drawn buggies and drays. We assumed that a war-caused shortage of gasoline accounted for the lack of motor cars. Since the air base, miles away at the other end of the island, was under an alert, there were no military personnel or cars this day.

Powers and I made our way to the largest structure in sight, the Grand Pacific Hotel, a two-story wooden building set among a small grove of palms. The lobby could have been the Hollywood version of a South Sea island set, complete with slowly revolving ceiling fans, tile floors and an elderly, walrus-mustached gentleman in a white linen suit, seated in a high-backed wicker chair reading a newspaper. In the adjacent bar, we were the only customers. The bartender, a thin white man in his fifties, stood polishing glasses when we entered. He glanced up. "Well if it isn't the United States Navy. Welcome, gents." He pronounced it "neighvey." Moments into our conversation he told us that he was a New Zealander who'd been in Fiji for twelve years. He fixed us tall tropic fruity drinks which had very little alcohol. "Perfect for this climate," he assured us. Many of the Fijian men, he told us, were in an army battalion in the Solomon Islands, at Bougainville and Guadalcanal, mopping up the remainder of the Japanese army who hid out in the hills.

We wondered about the large number of East Indians.

"The Fijians wouldn't do the dirty work—construction, road-building," said the bartender. "So the British brought the Indians here as indentured laborers in the eighteen-eighties." He chuckled. "We British imported the Indians to do our labor. Now they own the shops and businesses. We work for them."

I was curious about the medical facilities on the island.

"Well there's the Colonial Hospital." As an afterthought he added, "And the medical school."

Medical school?

He pointed. "Just up the hill. About a quarter mile."

Powers and I finished our drinks. He headed back to the ship while I decided to investigate the medical school.

Following the bartender's direction, I trudged up a road, passing a few wood shacks until a two-storied stucco structure came into view. The sign in front said: Colonial Memorial Hospital, but it did not look like any hospital I'd ever seen. A narrow structure, it consisted of two floors, each with about fifteen open balconies, some partially covered by canvas or some similar material. A low railing ran at the outer edge of each balcony, and although I couldn't see inside, I had the impression that each led to a patient's room.

Adjacent to the main hospital building was a long, gray, one-story wood and stucco building. As I passed the doorway at one end, I heard an English-speaking, male voice from within. I walked up to the entrance and peered inside to a classroom in which about twenty young, brown men sat in several rows facing me. They were barefoot and identically dressed in white sarongs and loose white, collarless shirts. The man who was speaking was white, wore khaki shorts and sat on a stool in front of the class with his back to me. When the students shifted their gazes to the doorway, he turned to face me. "How do you do," he said. "May I help you?" His English was cultured; he appeared to be in his mid-fifties, had a wiry build and was bald with a fringe of white hair. His narrow, clean-shaven face was lightly creased with smile lines.

"I'm looking for the medical school."

He nodded. "This is it." He glanced at the bronze oak leaf insignia pinned to my shirt collar. "Navy Medical Corps?"

"Yes. " I introduced myself. "I apologize for the intrusion. I see you're busy. I'll come back later."

I started to leave but he jumped down from the stool. "No, don't go, Doctor." He moved rapidly to where I stood and grabbed my elbow pulling me into the classroom. "I'm Dr. Hoodless." He swept an arm to encompass the class. "These are my students." Several smiled and nodded at the introduction.

Hoodless pointed to an anatomical chart hanging from a wall. "I'm just starting an anatomy lecture. Subject is the thoracic duct. Let me pop back to my office and fetch us some tea. While I'm gone why don't you start the lecture?"

Barry Friedman

Me? Lecture on the thoracic duct? When I had studied anatomy in my first year of medical school, the thoracic duct was little more than a footnote. I started to protest my ignorance but Hoodless was gone, leaving me to gaze blankly into the smiling faces of the class I'd suddenly inherited. The heat of the room rose a dozen degrees while I rapidly scrolled through my memory. What the hell could I say about it.?

I cleared my throat and pointed to the chart, fortunately labeled. An arrow led to a narrow tubular structure that extended upward alongside the spinal column from the lower trunk to the neck. There it disappeared into several large veins, also fortunately labeled. "The thoracic duct which you see here..." I walked slowly to the chart and looked around for a pointer—anything to give me time to think. One of the students leapt from his chair, retrieved a long wooden pointer from the chalk tray and pushed it into my hand.

Suddenly, I found filed away in the recesses of my brain, the picture of a patient I'd attended while I was an intern on emergency service. He'd been involved in a barroom brawl, and was brought to the ER with a stab wound of the neck.

I described the scene, embellishing it, and could see the students intently hanging on my words. "There was surprisingly little blood; the jugular vein and carotid artery, which are here... and here..." I tapped the chart on the appropriate structures, "... had mi-

Survivor

raculously been spared. But—," I paused, really getting into it now. "I saw oozing from the wound a yellowish, thin, serous fluid."

I stopped and waved the pointer at the class. "Can anyone tell me what the fluid could be?" Now I was Socrates in the Agora, a group of young Platos at my feet.

A hand shot in the air. "Lymphatic fluid?"

"Right! Where does the fluid come from?"

Several hands rose. I selected one. The student stood like a soldier at attention. "Sir! From the lymph nodes. They drain lymph into thoracic duct. Sir!" He plopped back into his chair.

These young men knew more about the subject than I did.

For the next few minutes, I related in the goriest terms I could muster, how a surgical resident and I had explored the wound, found that the thoracic duct had been severed and repaired it with fine sutures.

By now I had exhausted my scanty knowledge, and while I was trying to think of an act I could perform for an encore, I was relieved to see Dr. Hoodless returning with a tray.

"You've been an attentive audience," I said. "I hope I've added something to your knowledge."

The students snapped their fingers—in applause, I hoped.

Dr. Hoodless thanked me and dismissed the class.

Barry Friedman

After the students had filed out, we sat in two of the chairs they had vacated, and on another chair between us, Hoodless placed the tray containing two half coconut shells partly filled with hot tea.

"Tell me about the school," I said.

He took a sip of tea then patted his lips with a handkerchief. "As you see, this is a native medical school. It's been here since 1884."

I was amazed that it had been in existence longer than many medical schools in the States. "Where do the students come from?"

"The neighboring islands. Not only other islands in the Fiji group, but Samoa, Tonga, Gilberts, Ellis, any number of Pacific islands. In the beginning, missionaries who established schools on many of the islands, selected the brightest students and sent them here. Now the selection is done by competitive examinations. After these young men learn the basics of diagnosis and treatment, they return to their native islands as practitioners of medicine"

"How long is the course?"

"Four years."

"Four years! That's as long as my own medical school course."

Hoodless nodded. "By the time they're finished, these native medical practitioners, as we call them, are able to take care of most of the health needs of their villages—even minor surgical procedures, such as draining infections, removing embedded foreign bodies, su-

Survivor

turing lacerations, and the like. They give injections for treating yaws and vaccinations against smallpox. For more serious problems, they ship their patients to hospital here in Suva."

I wondered about the teaching staff.

Hoodless smiled. "You're looking at it."

"You mean you do all the teaching?"

He explained that he was the only full time tutor. "Before the war, we had about fourteen honorary lecturers and teachers, mostly medical people who served on the staff of the Colonial Hospital here. Most have gone off to war—in the New Zealand, Australian, British armies. So, I'm left with the job—with the help of a few physicians who are still around, and the odd visitor like yourself."

I was curious as to how Hoodless happened to be here.

"I'm a New Zealander," he said. "As you may know, Fiji is under the protection of New Zealand. I've been posted here by the British Colonial Government for more than ten years."

I noticed, tacked to a wall, a newspaper clipping showing a photograph of Amelia Earhart. In 1937 Miss Earhart and her navigator were on the final leg of a flight around the world in her small plane when contact with it was lost somewhere over the South Pacific. At the time, among the theories proposed were that the plane had gone down somewhere off Howland Island; or it had landed on one of the small islands held by the Japanese, and she and the navigator, suspected of spying, were executed.

"Is there a story connected with that picture? " I said.

Hoodless grinned. "One of the students put it up a year or two ago. I suppose I should take it down." He gazed at the clipping for a few seconds. "The 'story,' if it deserves the label, is that about two years ago, in early 1941, the British High Commissioner for the Pacific sent me a partial human skeleton and asked me to examine it. The bones had been found by one of their work parties on an uninhabited island belonging to the Republic of Kiribati, about 400 miles southwest of Howland Island. Since Howland had been on Miss Earhart's flight course, they postulated that the skeleton might be hers. Although the shape of the skull appeared consistent with that of a person of European rather than Polynesian descent, my measurements of the long bones and the shape of the pelvis indicated that they were most likely those of a male. End of story."

"I recall that she had a male navigator with her. Could the remains have been his?"

Hoodless shrugged. "A possibility, but..."

So, Amelia Earhart's disappearance remained a mystery.

I rose to leave when I thought of something that had puzzled me: Why had Hoodless been teaching the students about the thoracic duct, a relatively insignificant structure?

Hoodless nodded when I posed the question. "Insignificant to you, perhaps, but one of the endemic diseases of this area is filariasis. As practitioners, they will be treating patients with the condition."

Survivor

Of course. Filariasis, a tropical worm infestation, causes blockage of the lymphatic channels, of which the thoracic duct is the major vessel. If the duct is dammed, the parts of the body from which lymph would be drained, become greatly swollen. The condition is called elephantiasis, and I recalled a picture in my textbook of tropical medicine showing a man with filariasis whose scrotum was so swollen, he had to cart it in a wheelbarrow when he walked.

I shook Hoodless's hand and told him how much I had enjoyed our conversation. "My ship doesn't leave for another day." I said. "I know you're somewhat isolated. Do you need anything I can give you?"

He thought for a moment. "I haven't received my British Journal of Medicine for almost a year. I'm hungry for any news of what's happening in the medical world. If you have any old journals you'd be willing to dispose of, I would appreciate having them."

"I have a number of old issues of the Journal of the American Medical Association," I said. "If you can put up with news from one of the former British colonies, you're welcome to them."

He laughed. "I assume they're written in a language I can understand. Yes, I would love to have them."

Next day, laden with an armful of journals, I made my way to the school. Hoodless was overjoyed to have them, and as I prepared to leave, said, "Before you go, the class and I would like to present you with a small token of our appreciation."

Barry Friedman

He handed me two certificates. One proclaimed me "...an honorary member of the faculty of the Native Medical School of Fiji." The other was a license authorizing me to practice medicine in the Fiji Islands.

Ten years later, on a February day in Cleveland, Ohio where I was in practice, the temperature hovered around zero degrees Fahrenheit, and with the wind gusting off Lake Erie, the chill factor made it seem ten degrees colder. I had slogged through ankle-deep snow to my car in the hospital parking lot. The windshield was solidly coated with a sheet of ice, and for the third time that week, I had to hold a match to the car door key to defrost the lock. As I drove home, skidding and yawing on the icy roadway, my thoughts longingly strayed to a trunk in my attic in which I had stored mementos. Among them—that license to practice in Fiji.

Survivor

Chapter 25

In October 1943 Wellington, New Zealand teemed with servicemen of all ethnic and national affiliations. *Russell* arrived to escort transports carrying 18,600 Marines from the 2d Marine Division and the V Amphibious Corps spearheaded by the 2d Marine Regiment. Although at the time of *Russell's* arrival the destination of the troops was known only to the high command, it turned out to be Tarawa in the Gilbert Islands.

New Zealand and Australia were ideal liberty ports for the military serving in the South Pacific.

Gordon McCready wrote *in World War 2 People'sWar: An archive of World War Two2 memories-written by the public, gathered by BBC*

> "They (the Marines) arrived to a city where most eligible men were fighting the war in North Africa. Very rapidly, the relative wealth of the Marines and their access to "goodies" - silk stockings, chocolate made them attractive to men-starved 'Kiwi' girls.

Barry Friedman

"US servicemen arrived to take the NZ girl out with flowers, chocolates and stockings in one hand and a ground sheet over the other arm. With the return of the NZ military men in 1943, relationships between the two allied forces deteriorated rapidly. 'The Yank's were oversexed, overpaid and over here' was the derogatory response to the Marines.

"NZ servicemen composed a derogatory version of the 'Marine Hyme':

From the halls of Montezuma to the shores of Tripoli;
Their a pack of Yanky barstards for reasons plain to see;
They think they run New Zealand, but they couldn't run la-
trines;
Yet their F....g all our women, the United States Marines!"

The day following our arrival, Charlie Hart, *Russell's* Executive Officer and I took a tour bus to explore the countryside. New Zealand consists of a North and South Island. Wellington is located at the southern tip of North Island.

We headed south toward Christchurch, the largest city on the South Island. Once out of the city, we past miles of rocky hills reminiscent of some parts of upstate New York. The difference, however, was that here the hills were dotted with grazing sheep, more sheep in one place than I thought existed on the planet.

Our last and most interesting stop was at a Maori village.

Survivor

The Maori are the native or indigenous Polynesian people of NewZealand. They arrived in New Zealand from eastern Polynesia in the 14th Century.

There we were treated to the Haka or war dance. Traditionally, men dressed only in loin cloths, short spear-like structures coming out of their heads like horns, would perform Haka before a battle. The flashing eyes, outthrust tongues and warlike gestures of the warriors would strike fear into the hearts of their enemies.

Sightseeing was interesting, but liberty in this fascinating country demanded more action. One evening, with two other *Russell* officers I went out "on the town," ending with a visit to a tavern filled with cigarette smoke and a contingent of boisterous U.S. Marines. Hanging on their arms were Kiwi girls they had met at a USO dance. Waving the smoke from my eyes, I spied a familiar face: Marine First Lieutenant Mel Seltzer who had been my college fraternity brother. Mel had arrived in Wellington several weeks before, following a stint on Guadalcanal. I hadn't seen him in more than six years and I remembered he was about to go into his family's business.

"Yeah," he said. "I was hunting for crocodile skins to manufacture women's handbags. On 'Canal the situation was reversed, the crocks were hunting for me."

He wasn't just kidding. The saltwater crocodiles in the Solomon Islands are the largest and most aggressive reptiles in existence. These animals are often over twenty feet long and attack humans that get too close.

After we reminisced, he introduced me to several of the young women. There was no special attachment between them and any of the Marines and Mel gestured, "Take your pick."

Annie was an attractive young woman in her early twenties who appeared shy and quiet in contrast to most of her compatriots. She worked as a secretary in a cigarette factory, and after we'd had a couple of beers, Annie said she had to go home, she had to go to work the next day. I'd had enough merrymaking, so I volunteered to take her home.

I bid goodbye to Mel Seltzer and wished him luck. I learned much later that although his luck held out through the Tarawa invasion, it ran out in July 1944. Mel was killed in the Battle for Tinian in the Mariana Islands.

When the taxi left Annie off, we made a date for dinner next day. She arrived late, breathless and apologetic at the restaurant because "I had to pick up my weekly screw." When she saw my raised eyebrows, she said, "Paycheck. I forgot you foreigners speak a different language."

We had a nice dinner but when I ordered shepherd's pie for dessert, Annie shook her head. "I don't think you want that for dessert."

"Why? I love pies."

"Lamb pie?"

Survivor

We really *did* speak a different language.

When I took her home she said, "On Sunday my parents and I are going to the races. Would you like to come along?"

I jumped at the invitation, and they picked me up at dockside where *Russell* was berthed. Their car, like many in Wellington, was some kind of midget, about half the size of any American car. We all managed to squeeze in and her father drove us to the track.

A seedy-looking guy who knew Annie's father, after we'd been introduced sidled up to me, cupped his hand over his mouth and whispered, "Cannonball in the next race. Bet ten-bob on the nose."

New Zealand's currency in 1943 was based on the British pound. Ten-bob, or shillings, was about one U.S. dollar.

I placed the bet with one of the several bookmakers who stood on raised platforms. He gave me a slip of paper on which was written something in a code I didn't understand.

Annie explained, "That's the number of your horse and the odds."

Before the war, I had been to races at Saratoga in upper New York State, so I was confused when I saw the horses line up at the start of this one. I soon learned that in contrast to the races in the States, in New Zealand they run counter-clockwise.

To my surprise and delight, Cannonball won as did two other tips he gave me. Either the races were fixed or this tout knew more about racehorses than most other people. I ended up winning the U.S.

equivalent of about sixty dollars. When I saw him before we left, I asked him how much I owed him.

He waved it off. "Nah. Tyke it with thanks to you Yanks for savin' our arses from the Japs."

But good times soon enough came to an end, and the first day of November 1943, we left New Zealand. After several days of drills for an amphibious landing, *Russell* joined up with transports, battleships, cruisers, and more than sixty destroyers. The armada was the largest so-far assembled in the Pacific. Their destination: Tarawa, an atoll in the Gilbert Islands.

The Japanese had occupied the Gilbert Islands since shortly after the Pearl Harbor attack 7 December 1941. They gradually increase their strength of the garrison, by expansion of the occupied area to include Tarawa Atoll in the Gilberts. Its strategic character changed from that of a lookout post to a fortified station.

Located about 2,400 miles southwest of Pearl Harbor, Betio is the largest islet in the Tarawa Atoll. Shaped roughly like a long, thin triangle, the tiny island is approximately two miles long. It is narrow, being only 800 yards wide at the widest point. It is barely 6 feet above sea level.

En route to the invasion, *Russell* made several sonar contacts. Apparently anticipating an attack, the Japanese had stationed half a dozen submarines along the perimeter of the island group. Their duty seemed to be surveillance since the convoy experienced no torpedo attacks, however *Russell* responded to the sonar contacts making depth charge attacks, one of which resulted in a mile-long diesel oil slick.

D-Day Tarawa, 20 November 1943. Aboard *Russell* the call to General Quarters came at 0430. We donned our helmets and life jackets and manned our battle stations. Alongside her as the ships made their way toward the atoll, were the battleships *Colorado* and *Maryland.* Around 0500, the ships standing offshore started bombarding the beaches which had been designated as landing zones for the troops. The din was ear-splitting as the massive 16-inch cannons of the battleships belched forth tons of shells. Although *Russell's* 5-inchers were dwarfed by comparison, their fire was more rapid, raining the decks with their ash. For three hours the bombardment went on, causing explosions on the target areas, illuminating the sky. At first, there were several volleys of return fire from the beach, but they caused no damage to the ships, and they soon ceased, the inference being that the enemy guns had been knocked out of action.

By 0900 when the Marines began loading into Higgins boats for the invasion, the feeling aboard *Russell* and expressed by many was, "No one could have survived that bombardment. They must all be dead."

The first indication of how wrong we were came with radioed distress calls from the landing craft.

Barry Friedman

Robert Sherrod, a war correspondent, was with a contingent of Marines who boarded a landing craft for the landing. His eye witness account from the standpoint of one who went ashore, was published in *Tarawa: the Story of a Battle* (1944.) Parts of his description are in an article entitled, *The Bloody Battle of Tarawa. 1943* and can be found in *Eyewitness to History,www.eyewitnesstohistory.com* (2003) It is excerpted here:

At 0635, Sherrod and a 30-man, Marine assault force board a Higgins landing craft and head for the enemy beach. It takes an hour and a half for the landing craft to reach its rendezvous point off the beach where it joins other assault boats for the landing

It is here that Sherrod gets his first warning that something is going terribly wrong with the attack. He can see no landing craft on the beach—our assault waves should have previously gone ashore. At this point, the commander of the landing craft announces that he can go no further as the water is too shallow. The assault team will have to transfer to a tank-like amphtrack for the rest of the journey. We rejoin Sherrod's account as the Marines scramble aboard the amphtrack under intense enemy machinegun fire:

"We jumped into the little tractor boat and quickly settled on the deck. 'Oh God, I'm scared' said the little Marine, a

Survivor

telephone operator, who sat next to me forward in the boat. I gritted my teeth and tried to force a smile that would not come and tried to stop quivering all over (now I was shaking from fear). I said, in an effort to be reassuring, 'I'm scared, too.' I never made a more truthful statement in all my life.

"Now I knew, positively, that there were Japs, and evidently plenty of them, on the island. They were not dead. The bursts of shellfire all around us evidenced the fact that there was plenty of life in them!

"After the first wave there apparently had not been any organized waves, those organized waves which hit the beach so beautifully in the last rehearsal. There had been only an occasional amphtrack which hit the beach, then turned around (if it wasn't knocked out) and went back for more men. There we were: a single boat, a little wavelet of our own, and we were already getting the hell shot out of us, with a thousand yards to go. I peered over the side of the amphtrack and saw another amphtrack three hundred yards to the left get a direct hit from what looked like a mortar shell.

"'It's hell in there,' said the amphtrack boss, who was pretty wild-eyed himself. 'They've already knocked out a lot of amphtracks and there are a lot of wounded men lying on the beach. See that old hulk of a Jap freighter over there? I'll let you out about there, then go back to get some more men.

Barry Friedman

You can wade in from there.' I looked. The rusty old ship was about two hundred yards beyond the pier. That meant some seven hundred yards of wading through the fire of machine guns whose bullets already were whistling over our heads.

"The fifteen of us—I think it was fifteen—scurried over the side of the amphtrack into the water that was neck-deep. We started wading.

"No sooner had we hit the water than the Jap machine guns really opened up on us. There must have been five or six of these machine guns concentrating their fire on us. It was painfully slow, wading in such deep water. And we had seven hundred yards to walk slowly into that machinegun fire, looming into larger targets as we rose onto higher ground. I was scared, as I had never been scared before. But my head was clear. I was extremely alert, as though my brain were dictating that I live these last minutes for all they were worth. I recalled that psychologists say fear in battle is a good thing; it stimulates the adrenalin glands and heavily loads the blood supply with oxygen.

"I do not know when it was that I realized I wasn't frightened any longer. I suppose it was when I looked around and saw the amphtrack scooting back for more Marines. Perhaps it was when I noticed that bullets were hitting six inches to the left or six inches to the right. I could have sworn that I

Survivor

could have reached out and touched a hundred bullets. I remember chuckling inside and saying aloud, 'You bastards, you certainly are lousy shots.'

"After wading through several centuries and some two hundred yards of shallowing water and deepening machinegun fire, I looked to the left and saw that we had passed the end of the pier. I didn't know whether any Jap snipers were still under the pier or not, but I knew we couldn't do any worse. I waved to the Marines on my immediate right and shouted, 'Let's head for the pier!' Seven of them came. The other seven Marines were far to the right. They followed a naval ensign straight into the beach—there was no Marine officer in our amphtrack. The ensign said later that he thought three of the seven had been killed in the water."

Except for some mopping up, the land battle was over on 23 November. It had lasted four days. Of more than 3,600 Japanese troops only seventeen lived to surrender. In addition, of 1,200 Korean laborers who had been brought in to construct defenses, only 129 survived.

On the American side, the 2nd Marine Division suffered 978 killed and almost 2,200 wounded. Most of the casualties occurred in the first few hours of the battle.

Barry Friedman

For months after Tarawa a number of influential people expressed their opinion as to whether the assault costing so many lives was worth it.

General Holland Smith was highly critical of the Navy. In his biography, he stated:

"Was Tarawa worth it? My answer is unqualified: No. From the very beginning the decision of the Joint Chiefs to seize Tarawa was a mistake and from their initial mistake grew the terrible drama of errors, errors of omission rather than commission, resulting in these needless casualties."

Admiral Chester Nimitz, Admiral Raymond Spruance, Lt General Julian Smith and Lt Colonel David Shoup disagreed with that assessment. Said Nimitz:

"The capture of Tarawa knocked down the front door to the Japanese defenses in the Central Pacific."

In the Marshalls campaign only 10 weeks after the seizure of Tarawa, aircraft from the airfield at Betio, part of the Tarawa atoll, proved invaluable. Of greater significance to success in the Marshalls were the lessons learned from the battle itself.

The losses at Tarawa resulted from a number of contributing factors, among which were the inability of a naval bombardment to weaken the defenses of a well entrenched enemy, the miscalculation of the tide and the height of the obstructing coral reefs, the operational short comings of the landing craft available, and the difficul-

Survivor

ties of coordinating and communicating between the different forces involved. It was the first time in the war that a United States amphibious landing was opposed by well entrenched, determined defenders. Previous landings, such as the landing at Guadalcanal, had been unexpected and met with little or no initial resistance. At the time, Tarawa was the most heavily defended atoll invaded by Allied forces in the Pacific.

Barry Friedman

Chapter 26

In April 1942, four months after the Pearl Harbor attack, military commanders were making plans to retake the Pacific Islands that the Japanese occupied. Admirals King and Nimitz represented the Navy's interest. The deliberations included General McArthur who had been evacuated by PT boat from Corregidor in the Philippines and was now in Australia. He was in charge of the ground forces in the Southwest Pacific. The first of the Japanese-held islands was Guadalcanal, then working their way north, the Gilbert Islands of which Tarawa was the principal target for the next stage. Next on the agenda was the Marshall Islands.

The Marshalls are a group of islands and atolls, one of which is Bikini, best known now as the site for nuclear bomb tests in 1946. Another is Kwajalein one of the world's largest coral atolls as measured by area of enclosed water.

Survivor

With Tarawa secured, *Russell* joined a carrier task force that included the new *Yorktown,* a carrier replacement for the *Yorktown* sunk in the Battle of Midway.

En route from the Gilbert Islands north to Pearl Harbor, the force carried out bombing and shelling attacks on Kwajalein and Wotje islands in the Marshall Island group. Although landing U.S. troops was not on the schedule for another two months, the lesson learned from Tarawa was that well-entrenched troops on the island were almost impossible to dislodge even with massive shelling. Yet, it was vital to inflict on the defenders whatever damage was possible before subjecting the U.S.troops who would make the landing, to gunfire from the beaches. While the carrier-based U.S. planes raked the beaches with bombs, *Russell* along with other warships in the task force poured tons of lead onto the landing zones.

Rough seas made launching and recovery of carrier planes difficult, keeping *Russell* busy with rescue operations. Four crew men from *Enterprise* planes were pulled from the water uninjured. Earlier the same day, three airmen from an *Essex* based torpedo plane had gone down, two of whom suffered gastrointestinal injuries when a depth charge the plane carried went off under them. The effect of the explosion was to drive water up their rectums like a high pressure enema. Although the injury was not life-threatening, the effects would be felt for weeks or months.

Barry Friedman

The Japanese retaliated to the raid by launching torpedo planes. Two were shot down by anti-aircraft fire from *Enterprise* and the cruiser *Baltimore*. However, the enemy was persistent sending two other waves of torpedo planes at the ships. Close to midnight, *Russell* radar picked up an approaching Japanese plane, and firing by radar control, made a direct hit when the plane was 4,000 yards away. The fireball that resulted dramatically lit up the night sky. Half an hour later, another plane was downed by *Russell's* guns.

Back in Pearl Harbor, two events awaited *Russell's* return. One was Captain McClain's promotion to Commander, a rank which gave him command of a larger ship. Second, was the arrival on board of Lieut. Cmdr Fredrick Shaw (not his real name) who was to relieve McClain as *Russell's* skipper.

Shaw had been in the Annapolis class ahead of McClain, but this was to be his first combat assignment. His previous wartime duty had been spent in Washington. Gaunt and dour-faced with cheeks so sunken you could see the outlines of his teeth through them, Shaw looked like a death camp survivor who had barely made it. Standing, he looked like the letter "s" (lower case). On the quarterdeck during the brief change-of-command ceremony, Shaw stood alongside Charlie Hart, the executive officer. There couldn't have been a more striking contrast in appearances. Hart was a straight-backed, sandy-haired guy whose clear blue eyes never wavered from your face while you

Survivor

talked to him. As I watched the two I wondered if they had both gone to the same Naval Academy.

I shook hands with McClain as he stood at the head of the gangway preparing to leave. "We'll miss you, Captain."

"You mean you'll miss taking more of my dough in cribbage." During long days at sea, the skipper and I relieved some of the boredom playing cribbage in his small cabin on the bridge. He went on, "Thanks for your sentiments, Doc. I'm going to miss all you guys. But a few weeks in the States should help dry my tears." McClain saluted the flag, sprinted down the gangway and disappeared into a jeep waiting for him at dockside.

The afternoon after Shaw came aboard, I sat in the wardroom drinking coffee with Hart. I said, "Charlie, you're an Annapolis man. Isn't it unusual for a guy who is regular Navy, like Shaw, to jockey a desk for over a year when there's a shooting war going on?"

Hart chewed on a roll before he answered. "There's probably a good reason."

I didn't press him. Charlie Hart was pleasant and efficient but spoke mostly in one-word sentences. By comparison, Gary Cooper, the cowboy movie star, was a chatterbox.

Ten minutes after I had put the question to Hart, I got the real answer. The wardroom phone rang. Stu Jardine, the bridge duty officer was on the line. "The Captain wants to see you in his cabin."

I rubbed my palms. "Great, another cribbage player."

I knocked on the Captain's cabin door. The voice that told me to come in was barely audible. Shaw lay on his bunk, hands folded across his chest. A lily and a casket were all that were needed to complete the picture. He stared blankly at the overhead. On the deck in his cabin were several open, empty suitcases.

"Did you send for me, sir?"

"Yes, Doctor. I'm having some stomach cramps. I'd like something to relieve them."

I wanted some more information before I dispensed any medicine. In spite of his moribund appearance, he didn't seem to be in pain when he took command a few hours before.

"This is a long story with me," he said. "I've had ulcers for years. That's why they wouldn't let me go to sea until now. I've got some antacids that I take regularly, but I thought maybe a sedative would help."

As he spoke he pointed to the desk on which were twenty or more medicine bottles of various sizes and colors. He had a larger supply of medicines than I had in sickbay. I examined several bottles and recognized barbiturate tablets and other medications commonly used for intestinal spasm. Many of the drugs I could not identify.

I picked up a bottle of phenobarbital from his desk. "Here, this is as good a sedative as any."

"I thought you might have something stronger."

Survivor

"The only thing I have that's stronger is morphine. But before I give you a narcotic I'll have to examine you completely."

He was silent for a moment. "Never mind. I'll get along with what I've got. I'll call you if I need anything else." He closed his eyes and I left the cabin.

Back in the wardroom Charlie Hart was still sitting where I had left him. "Charlie, I've just come from the Captain's quarters. He wanted some medicine. Did you know about his ulcers?"

Charlie shook his head. "He wouldn't have been sent to sea duty if there was anything seriously wrong with him."

I had to agree, but I felt uneasy.

Next day we had target practice off the tip of Hawaii, in rehearsal for our next operation the details of which were locked in a sealed envelope in the Captain's safe.

The drill consisted of firing our five-inch guns at designated areas on the island. Captain Shaw had spent most of the day sitting silently in his tall swivel stool on the bridge while the Executive Officer gave orders for maneuvering the ship and firing on the shore targets, duties usually carried out by the commanding officer. Periodically, the Captain peered at the target area through his binoculars. On several occasions, when our guns fired for long periods, Captain Shaw left his seat on the bridge and retired to his small bridge cabin behind the wheelhouse. After the firing stopped he returned to his seat where he sat without speaking.

Since I had no specific duties, I spent most of the day on the bridge watching the activity—and the Captain. Shaw's behavior seemed strange, and I watched the exec for his reaction. But he was preoccupied with giving orders to the helmsman and to the gunnery crew. If the Captain's actions disturbed him, he didn't show it.

That evening we returned to Pearl Harbor and docked alongside a destroyer tender, our "mother ship," from which we received our supplies. The Captain did not come down the wardroom for supper. Instead, he had a mess boy bring him a light snack which he ate alone in his cabin.

After supper I visited the medical department of the tender to pick up medical supplies and made arrangements to use their operating room the next morning. Since we had no operating room on our small ship, whenever we were in port with the tender, I scheduled minor elective operations such as excising cysts, unwanted tattoos, and similar procedures, in their operating room. As the only medical officer on our ship, I hungered for contact with other physicians, so these visits gave me the opportunity of chatting with the doctors on the tender.

The following morning as I prepared to board the tender to perform the surgery I had scheduled, I answered a page from the deck officer.

"The Captain wants to see you," he said. "He's in his cabin."

Survivor

I knocked on the door but there was no response. When I rapped louder and still received no answer, I opened the door and walked in. Captain Shaw, clad in pajamas, was lying on his bunk. His brow gleamed with beads of perspiration; his sweat-soaked hair was matted. His eyes were closed, and for a moment I thought he was unconscious. But when I stepped into the cabin, he opened his eyes. In a voice so low and hoarse I could barely make out the words, he said, "I'm sick."

"Does anything hurt?"

"Can't sleep…sick to my stomach…strange dreams."

Strange dreams? Bells went off in my head. I examined him thoroughly and found nothing abnormal: pulse, blood pressure, temperature all normal. This man was to be in command of our ship in a battle zone? Not on my watch; not on my ship; not if I could help it.

Today, Captain Shaw's condition would probably be called Acute Stress Disorder. If it lasts longer than a month, and is associated with physical or emotional trauma it would be classed as Posttraumatic Stress Disorder (PTSD.) During the First World War soldiers in combat who displayed incapacitating anxiety were said to be "Shell Shocked."

I said, "I think I'd better admit you to the hospital for a workup."

He seemed to brighten. "I think that would be best." His voice was stronger.

I called the Chief Medical Corpsman. "Andy, call Aiea Hospital and arrange to have Captain Shaw admitted this afternoon. I'll write the history and physical examination for his medical record when I finish our surgical cases. If Aiea wants to know the admitting diagnosis, it's 'Anxiety Neurosis'."

"Wow!"

"And keep it quiet. Let Mr. Hart know but no one else." I had to notify the exec. As second in command, he might have to assume the duties of Captain.

I crossed the gangway to the tender. The operating room was ready and I completed in two hours the operations I had scheduled. As I was changing from my scrub suit, Commander Gus Goetz, the tender's Senior Medical Officer, walked into the dressing rom. Gus was a big, likeable man who had been an orthopaedic surgeon in civilian life before the war.

He said, "Everything go all right?"

"Fine, Gus. Thanks for letting me use your OR."

"Any time. How long do you expect to be in Pearl?"

"The Admiral hasn't checked with me yet, but I'm going to ask for a month or two," I joked. "By the way, I'm admitting our skipper to Aiea this afternoon." Since Goetz was the senior physician of our destroyer squadron, I felt I should keep him informed.

He looked at me quizzically. "I never know when you're kidding. Are you serious?"

"Sure."

"What's wrong with him?"

Briefly, I told him what had happened.

Gus rolled his eyes. "Jesus, you can't remove the Captain of a ship from his post. You have to get permission from the Fleet Commander."

"How do I do that?"

"I'll call over to the Pacific Fleet office."

I returned to my ship to write the hospital admission note. Andy Anderson, my Chief Medical Corpsman had arranged to have me take Shaw to the Naval Hospital at Aiea Heights, overlooking Pearl Harbor.

"What about Mr. Hart. Did you notify him?" I said.

"He went ashore last night. He won't be back until this evening."

I was not looking forward to removing the Captain from the ship without notifying the Executive Officer, but I was not going to wait another full day. I checked Shaw in his quarters. He was sleeping, snoring loudly, and appeared more relaxed than at any time since he came on board. Maybe he's not so crazy after all, I thought.

Gus Goetz came aboard and met me in sickbay while I was writing the hospital admission note. He said, "Okay, it's all arranged. We're meeting with the Commander of the Pacific Destroyers and his staff this afternoon—and better wear a flak jacket. He didn't sound happy when I told him you were admitting your skipper."

Three hours later, Gus and I were ushered into the Pacific Fleet Headquarters. Seated around a long table were Rear Admiral M.S. Tisdale the Commander Destroyers Pacific Fleet and three members of his staff, a Captain, a commander and a lieut. commander. I was a lieutenant (jg), by several ranks the most junior officer in the room. The Admiral was a square-jawed man with a thin, Errol Flynn-type mustache, whose lips had a perpetual downturn. He squinted through narrowed eye slits as though peering through mist and wind.

It was apparent they had been discussing the Shaw case before we arrived. Without preliminary small talk the Admiral said, "Doctor, what do you have to tell us about Captain Shaw?"

I told them what had occurred since Shaw had come aboard the *Russell*. While I spoke the Admiral stared at me, hardly blinking. He tapped the table edge with the eraser end of a pencil. If his intension was to intimidate me, he succeeded. When I had finished speaking, he said, "What do you think is wrong with him?"

"He's acutely depressed."

The Admiral looked down, counting his fingers. "Isn't 'depression' a psychiatric diagnosis?"

"Yes sir."

He brought his head up sharply. I felt as though he was peering into the back of my skull. "Doctor, are you a psychiatrist?"

"No sir."

Survivor

"Then you aren't actually qualified to make a psychiatric diagnosis, are you?" Evidently I was on trial in this kangaroo court. No one but the Admiral had uttered a word since Gus and I entered the room. The Admiral was the prosecutor, the jury, and the judge.

I gazed at the ceiling, debating on an answer to his rhetoric question. There was no doubt in my mind that I was right. It didn't take a psychiatrist to know that Shaw was acutely depressed—but the Admiral didn't want to hear that. "No sir, I'm not a psychiatrist. That's why I'm admitting him to the hospital where someone who has more experience than I have, can examine and treat him."

"What is the expression you doctors use when you're not sure? Isn't it 'unknown diagnosis' or some such term?"

The Admiral had done some homework.

"Yes sir. The term is 'Diagnosis Unknown, Medical Observation'."

"Well, since you're not sure what his trouble is, that's the diagnosis you should use for Captain Shaw."

"Is that what you want me to do?"

"That's what I want you to do." His jaw seemed to jut out six inches from the rest of his face as he said it. He would get no argument from me. All I wanted was to end this inquisition and get the hell out of there.

"Aye, aye sir," I replied, like a good little sailor boy.

The Admiral stood and chairs scraped as everyone in the room jumped to his feet.

On the way back to our ships, Gus Goetz, who had been a silent observer during the proceedings, said, "I'd like to get that son-of-a-bitch as a patient and see if he takes orders as well as he gives them."

I shrugged. "Oh well, maybe that's how you win wars."

By the time we reached the ship, Captain Shaw was packed and ready to go. A jeep had been sent to the dock and we were driven to Aiea Naval Hospital. As we drove up to the entrance, a Captain in the Medical Corps greeted us. I had met him several months before. He was Executive Officer of the hospital. A feisty little man, the XO was a regular Navy physician, in contrast to most of the physicians in the wartime Navy, like myself, who were Naval Reserve officers, he had been in the Navy since his graduation from medical school, 25 years before.

He escorted us to the admitting office where we left Shaw to go through the admitting process. The XO beckoned me to follow him to his office and asked for Shaw's medical record. He read the note I had written and glanced up, his brow furrowed. "The diagnosis in your record says, 'Diagnosis Unknown, Medical Observation'. I don't get it. Your corpsman told me he has an anxiety neurosis."

"I'm sure he is in an acute depressed state, but the Admiral didn't want him admitted with that diagnosis—and the Admiral's got several more stripes on his sleeve than I do," I said.

Survivor

The XO's face reddened. "Screw the Admiral! Those Academy buddies are interested only in covering each other's ass. If he's got an anxiety neurosis, by God, that's going to be his admitting diagnosis!"

He tore out the page on which I had written the diagnosis. Calling a yeoman into his office, he said, "I want you to type another diagnosis page for this chart. The doctor here will tell you what to put down." He walked out of the room muttering curses.

Three days later, the *Russell,* with a new Captain hastily recruited from an officer pool, left Pearl Harbor. We were part of a task force bound for the invasion of Kwajalein, an atoll in the Marshall Islands, a Japanese stronghold from which planes had been attacking our ships. Shaw, I learned later, sailed in the opposite direction, destination Washington, D.C., a stronghold of a different kind.

Barry Friedman

Chapter 27

The new skipper of *Russell* was Lieutenant Commander Lewis R. Miller. A native of Gonzales, Texas, Captain Miller was an Annapolis graduate Class of 1926.In the early 1930s he had served aboard a Yangtze River gunboat. In 1942 he assumed command of the destroyer *USS Plunkett* and guided the ship through operations in the Atlantic, and took part in the invasion of Solerno, Italy.

In December 1943 he was in the officer's pool at Pearl Harbor awaiting assignment when he was tapped for command of *Russell.*

Although he was 38-years-old, Miller appeared to be ten years older. He gave orders in a quiet but authoritative tone with a Texas drawl. In his "Old China Hand" vernacular, the Executive Officer was "Mate,"gunnery officer was "Guns," ship's doctor was "Surg."

For the first few weeks after taking command, Captain Miller said little but observed everything through hooded eyes, contemplatively rubbing his chin, while sucking on a pipe stem. Then he expressed his dissatisfaction with the performance of the crew in a memorandum entitled "How We Fight."

Survivor

"This memorandum is for the information of all hands with the hope that it will help each man to see how he fits into the team and how important is the seemingly small part he is playing, Many will read this and have a surge of enthusiasm, and then relapse into dopey ways when they find that eternal vigilance is hard work.

"We have this destroyer, a ship which is always out in front. We first stand the full strength of the enemy attack, and we lead off the attack on him. There is nothing which is under the water, on the surface or in the skies which we do not attack. No other type ship or plane is so versatile, nor is so much expected from any craft which floats or flies.

"Now let us take stock of the *Russell*. She has a hull strong enough to keep out the seas, but nothing in the way of a structure which will stop even a rifle bullet. She is fast— about as fast as any. She has eight torpedoes which will sink anything which will float provided we can get them in. She has five-inch guns which will bring down a plane, sink a cruiser or anything smaller, and raise hell with a battleship provided they are smartly handled. The 40 mm guns will take any plane within two miles, stop a destroyer or cruiser, puncture a submarine so she can't submerge, and clear the topside of any ship. The 20 mm can take any plane within one mile, stop a destroyer, ruin a submarine's saddle tanks, and mow down topside personnel on any ship. The depth charges will crush a submarine's hull, or blow him to the surface where the guns can finish him off; they can also stop a ship close aboard, or can send the Bushido boys in the water who won't surrender, to the land where we won't have to fight them again.

"Now how can we best use this? It is easy to see that we are equipped to dish it out only. We weren't built to take it. **In order to win we must hit first with all we have.** This depends on you. Our effectiveness and survival depends on you being faster and more skillful than the enemy.

"This ship's company right now is not fast enough or skillful enough to last a hard fight. The lookouts are six blind mice. In five attempts at surprise fire the guns shot only twice and then didn't hit. Two times someone had turned off the power and once the gun would not operate. This won't do. The Gun Captain should have been checking up every minute to be sure everything was O.K. and the gun was ready to shoot. He should have had men watching the sky and the water, and especially one man looking into the sun with sunglasses; he should have been tracking and reporting it, and having a hard time keeping that old itchy trigger finger still. Another gun crew was taking a sunbath while a plane with a

Survivor

sleeve was in firing position. When told to wake up, the Gun Captain explained indignantly that nobody warned him. Son, the enemy never warns you. He loves to kill you in your sleep.

"On a destroyer, there are only two classes of people. The quick and the dead. Take your choice. Remember, it's hard work to be quick.

"When we make a torpedo attack use the individual target method if not told otherwise. Use one degree spread. If the target is bigger than a destroyer, fire all eight torpedoes. If you see a sub on the surface or at periscope depth, train on him and report ready to fire using local tube control. Never let the ship go down without firing torpedoes if there is an enemy ship near. If you don't get orders and it looks as if she is going to sink, fire them without orders using the best setup you can get. When a torpedoman has done that and set all the depth charges on safe, he is ready to go swimming, but not before that.

"When we attack a sub the soundman must cross the target, giving right and left cut ons. Otherwise we shall attack wakes. When the recorder is cut in I must get ranges and relative speeds in a steady flow. When the time comes I shall order, 'Fire on the recorder.' Or 'Fire so many seconds ahead (or behind) the recorder.' The officer running the recorder will

then take over and order the depth charges released at the ordered time. After all the charges are gone, I will turn 45 degrees toward the target, run for one minute and forty-five seconds on this course, then turn to the reverse of the attack
course for another run. During the 45 degree turn the soundman must regain contact. All ready guns of whatever caliber,
train on the depth charge explosions and watch the explosions
through your sights. If a sub comes up, let him have it with no
orders to open fire. During these turns the depth charge personnel will have about four minutes to reload all I-guns and
report them ready to fire. Can you do it? If not, let me know,
because you must. If you need help, you will get it.

"When any planes are in the air, track them. If one starts
to come in or comes within range, being identified as enemy,
I shall order 'Commence firing on plane bearing such and
such.' If you have been tracking you have a setup and the first
salvo should come a fraction of a second after the order is
given. If you see one that I have missed, report him and ask to
open fire. If he is already coming at you spitting venom, let
him have it without orders.

"When we go into action against surface ships, track
your target, or if none has been designated, the nearest enemy
ship. The words 'Commence firing!' should just leave my
mouth before the first salvo.

Survivor

"Remember, it isn't all right if something doesn't work, it's a stitch in your *die sack*. It isn't all right if the gun isn't ready to shoot right now because someone turned off the power or the mechanism won't work—it's a bullet in your guts. It isn't all right that you are sunbathing instead of tracking because someone didn't warn you—it's a bomb right down your neck.

"Take your choice—be quick or dead, but remember it's hard work being quick.

(Signed) L.R.Miller

Lieutenant Commander USN

Commanding Officer

Chapter 28

With each engagement in the Pacific War, the size of the invading force increased in size. When *Russell* left Pearl Harbor for the Marshall Island assault, it joined an armada that stretched over the visible horizon.

At dawn on 30 January 1943, D-Day minus two, *Russell* in company with heavy cruisers *Louisville*, *Mobile*, and *Santa Fe*, and five other destroyers sailed into sight of a low-lying, comma-shaped island. Like the others in the Marshall group, Wotje Island was narrow, flat and about two miles long. It rose about twenty feet above sea level. A wooded area consisting of coconut palms, breadfruit trees, and scrub pines was surrounded by a wide beach and coral reef. The Japanese had constructed an airstrip on Wotje which was used as a seaplane base.

At 0600, standing off shore, *Russell* alongside *Louisville* started raking the island with gunfire. Large explosions erupted, presumably from fuel storage tanks. After an hour of constant bombardment, return fire from batteries on the island splashed into the seas around the ships. One volley straddled the cruiser *Biloxi,* but the shore gun was silenced before any damage was done.

Russell moved out of range of the shore batteries, leaving the *Louisville* to continue blasting the airstrip with her 8-inch guns. After four hours of shelling, Wotje was covered with smoke from one end of the island to the other.

The following day, D-Day minus one, *Russell* shifted to an island in the northern part of the Marshalls, Roi-Namur. There, she screened the battleship *Maryland* while she poured tons of shells into the island in preparation for landing the next day by Marines of the 4th Division. Even though the *Russell* was several hundred yards from the battleship, the din was deafening. While it was hard to imagine that any of Japanese defenders could survive the bombardment, sporadic return fire from shore emplacements demonstrated that at least some were still capable of resisting. One salvo from the island splashed 100 feet behind *Russell's* stern causing anxiety but no structural damage.

In order to direct fire from the ships to target shore batteries, the cruiser *Santa Fe* launched a scout plane. After it had done its work, the plane returned but in attempting to land, crashed into the sea. *Russell* responded to the call for rescue and plucked the sodden plane crew out of the water. After they were hauled aboard, I examined them and determined that except for minor cuts and bruises, they had sustained no serious injuries.

Captain Miller then turned his attention to the floating remains of the plane. Since it represented a potential hazard to the navigating vessels, he ordered the 20 mm and 40 mm gun crews to open fire on the hulk. It was distressing to watch while several million dollars of U.S. money disintegrated and plunged into the depths of the Pacific.

D-Day, 1 February, the call to General Quarters was sounded at 0500. From then until the amphibious craft carrying the invading Marines headed for the island, *Russell* poured shell after shell on the beaches designated as landing zones. The fear that troops would be mowed down by well-entrenched gun emplacements like those at Tarawa, proved to be ill-founded. They met little resistance and the worst casualties occurred when a Marine demolition team threw a satchel charge of high explosives into a Japanese bunker which turned out to be a torpedo warhead magazine. The resulting explosion killed twenty Marines and wounded dozens more. Only 51 of the original 3,500 Japanese defenders of Roi-Namur survived to be captured.

At the same time the Marines were landing on Roi, troops of the Army's 7th Infantry Division prepared for landing on Kwajalein Island. The bombardment by battleships and B-24 bombers from Apamama, was devastating. One observer stated that "the entire island looked as if it had been picked up 20,000 feet and then dropped." In addition, for the first time combined Army-Navy underwater demolition teams were used to search the beaches for un-

Survivor

derwater obstacles and mines. In the case of Kwajalein, none were found

By the time the 7th Division landed on Kwajalein Island there was little resistance; by night the Americans estimated that only 1,500 of the original 5,000 defenders were still alive.

By D-Day plus one, *Russell* received reports that the Marshall Island invasion was declared secured and the ship entered the huge Kwajalein lagoon. But the tired old girl was showing the effects of more than two years of Pacific war on top of her previous Atlantic service. The ship's after engine broke down and one sonar unit became inoperable. It took a week for temporary repairs to be made, just in time to escort six transports to Pearl Harbor.

Although the casualties to American troops were substantial, compared to the Guadalcanal and Tarawa campaigns, the Marshall Islands invasion was accomplished with relative ease.

Chapter 29

While *Russell* personnel were focused on the South Pacific War in April and May 1944, the rest of the world watched events in Europe in anticipation of an Allied invasion of German-held France. Reconnaissance by aerial photos was providing a mosaic of the French English Channel coast to help General Dwight Eisenhower determine the most desirable sites for a landing. Hundreds of Flying Fortress bombers were now pounding major German cities daily with little opposition from German fighter planes although anti-aircraft fire still accounted for some U.S. losses.

In contrast to the early days of the war, Atlantic convoys were now delivering supplies to Great Britain with only sporadic U-Boat attacks.

Allied troops had conquered most of Italy, which was allied with Germany, and the Russian Army had thrown back the Germans who had penetrated the Russian homeland. The Russians were now the aggressors and were closing in on Germany from the east.

Survivor

In the United States some rationing was eased, although commodities which had any relevance to the war were not available to the public. Because of the need for military combat manpower, the Army ordered a 50-percent cutback of medical school admissions in spite of warnings that the action would result in severe shortage of doctors for some time in the future.

In India, Mahatma Gandhi was released after almost two years of incarceration. He had been imprisoned in 1942 for proposing that India yield to the Japanese without a fight. His views were expressed not because he was in sympathy with the Axis powers, but because they were in concert with his life-long preaching as a pacifist.

In *Russell's* charthouse, Lieutenant William Bargeloh, who had succeeded Charlie Hart as Executive Officer, was plotting the ship's course toward New Guinea where the ship would spend the better part of the next twelve months. General Douglas McArthur commanded the Allied forces in the southwest Pacific from south of the Solomon Islands to Australia. Ships assigned to the area, as was *Russell*, were referred to as "McArthur's Navy."

New Guinea was the world's second largest island after Greenland. Its north coastline extends nearly 1,600 miles from twelve degrees south latitude to just south of the equator; from Milne Bay and Port Moresby on the eastern end to Sansapor at the western end. A major mountain range cuts across the island's center and makes passage overland through the jungled mountains nearly impossible. On New Guinea's north side, scene of most of the ground fighting during 1942-1945, rainfall runs as high as 300 inches per year.

Disease thrived on New Guinea. Ground troops suffered malaria, dengue fever, dysentery, scrub typhus, and a host of other tropical sicknesses. Scattered, tiny coastal settlements dotted the north coastline, but inland the lush tropical jungle swallowed men and equipment.

Fed by the frequent downpours, the lush rain-forest jungle afforded excellent concealment to stubborn Japanese defenders who could harass Allied troops on the coast and then retreat into the jungle.

In 1942, the Japanese attempted to invade Port Moresby to isolate Australia about 500 miles to the south, but they were repulsed by the Australian Army. The Japanese did establish bases in several north coastal settlements on New Guinea including Aitope and Hollandia, and on Wadke and Biak Islands, off the New Guinea coast.

By the time *Russell* arrived in New Guinea on 5 May 1944, units of the Australian Army had cleared the Japanese from Aitope and Hollandia. Three weeks later, she stood off shore at Biak Island, bombarding the beaches with her 5-inch shells in preparation for an amphibious landing by U.S. Army troops.

The enemy did not give up the island easily, and although the Battle of Biak Island is now a little more than a footnote in the histo-

Survivor

ry of the Pacific War, the troops suffered substantial casualties. Daily air attacks on ships of the invading force kept the *Russell* gunners busy.

It was during the Biak island campaign that I met Tadashi Harada for only fifteen seconds—the last fifteen seconds of his life. But the memory of him has remained with me.

That hazy morning in early June, 1944, I leaned on a wing of the bridge, mesmerized as the bow cleaved through the gentle swells, raising a small wave first on one side then the other as the ship cruised a zig-zag pattern toward a landing area on the beach. About one-hundred yards off our starboard a group of flat-faced landing craft slapped through the water. As the small craft dipped into valleys between swells, I caught a glimpse of khaki helmets on the troops packed inside. For some this would be a one-way trip. Behind me, through the open door of the wheelhouse I heard the incessant static of the ship-to-ship radio, crackling messages, wondering who understood the gibberish. Every few minutes the Captain, seated in his high stool facing the bridge windshield, droned a change-of-course order, echoed by the helmsman.

"Just like any day at the office, right, Doc?"

I didn't have to look up. The voice of Lieut. Bill Bargeloh, the Executive Officer, standing next to me, came from deep in his throat and rolled around his tongue before it released as a West Virginia drawl. He raised his binoculars and slowly scanned the horizon. A blondish cowlick peeked beneath the edge of his campaign cap. Bargeloh's wiry frame was in constant motion, small athetoid-like movements. He peered through the lenses, turning one way then the other.

"Too quiet," he said. "Something's gonna happen."

A moment later, it did.

From the wheelhouse came the excited voice of the crewman who relayed messages between the radar room and the bridge. "Bogies!"

As many times as I'd heard the AWWWK of the general quarters alarm, it never failed to make small insects crawl up my back. My chest tightened as I flew down the ladder to the main deck. I dodged crewmen, helmets askew, sprinting to their battle stations while they reached behind to find the armholes of their bulky life jackets. I got to the wardroom door as one of the crew was getting ready to spin the wheel that sealed the compartment. I yelled, "Hold it! I've got to get my gear."

I ran to my stateroom, grabbed my helmet, life jacket and a canvas pack containing bandages, gauze, tape and morphine syrettes. I started out the door, realized I'd forgotten the moving picture camera and went back to retrieve it.

With my first aid kit slung over one shoulder and the camera over the other, I ran back to the bridge.

Survivor

"Two bogies at oh-seven-four, distance..." In the wheelhouse, a crewman wearing a headphone stood behind the Captain reporting what the radarman had detected on his screen.

"Flank speed ahead." The Captain's crisp order was repeated by one of the crewmen into his headphone. Within seconds, I could feel the throb of the deck underfoot, the surge as we powered forward. At the same time the ship began circling evasively. On either wing of the bridge, stood an officer, binoculars raised to his eyes, searching. In the distance, the low clouds suddenly were peppered with small black puffs. Moments later came the staccato explosions of anti-aircraft fire.

I glanced at Bargeloh. "Where's the AA coming from?"

"Beach maybe. *Reid's* in that direction too."

Later we learned it was the *Reid*, another destroyer in our group that had come under attack by a group of Japanese planes and was firing back.

"Bogies dead ahead!" The shout came from one of the visual spotters on the bridge.

The five-inch gun turrets swung around, muzzles pointed to the sky and the roar of their fire made my eardrums ache. The 20-millimeter guns added their chatter to the deafening noise. A hundred yards astern, the *Mustin* joined the thundering chorus. The sky above was now blackened with exploding shells. The smell of cordite stung my nostrils.

Peering through the smoky haze that now enveloped the ship, I caught a glimpse of two specks darting through the clouds. One headed for the beach area and dove out of sight. The other seemed to stop, change direction and speed up, like a water skate on a clear pond. Then, trailing black smoke it slowly glided toward the water.

Someone shouted, "We got him!"

Through the eyepiece of my camera, I watched the wounded plane. It was still high in the air descending in a steep glide, when what appeared to be a puff of white smoke separated from it.

Bargeloh was watching through his binoculars. "He's bailed out."

I realized that the white puff was a parachute.

Our guns were now quiet. All around me on the bridge, below on the main deck, crewmen stood in silent fascination as the parachute floated toward the sea.

In the wheelhouse, the Captain ordered a course heading for the spot it appeared the chute would land. "Get ready to haul him aboard," he told the Exec.

Bargeloh scurried down the ladder to the main deck, I followed on his heels. As he ran, he flipped up the cover on his sidearm holster. His hand rested on the grip of his pistol.

The parachute was about five hundred feet in the air and several hundred yards in front of our bow, when a plane darted from the clouds followed a moment later by another. The wing markings were

Survivor

clear, Aussies. One of the planes dove toward the descending chute spitting red tracers. In a moment both planes were gone, in the direction of the beach.

By now we could make out the tiny dark form swinging below the billowing parachute. As it descended, it drifted towards us. The Captain maneuvered the ship, keeping the chute over our bow. Within minutes the parachute lay flat on the surface of the water and we were alongside. Floating face down was the airman.

One of the crewmen standing alongside the rail shouted, "He moved his arm!"

Bargeloh ordered everyone to stand back while one of the crewmen manned a long boat hook. He fished in the water with the hook until he engaged several of the parachute shrouds, and with three other sailors tugging, they hauled the airman up and over the deck rail. Several others pulled in the huge silk chute.

The sodden khaki-clad figure lay prone on the deck. He was small, almost feminine. He still wore his leather aviator helmet, goggles pushed up on his forehead. Someone drew a large hunting knife and started sawing away at the shrouds that held the airman to the parachute.

Bargeloh said, "Is he alive, Doc?"

I moved in to see. An arm twitched. Someone behind me said, "He's moving!" I bent forward. A huge hole in the middle of his chest was surrounded by shredded fibers of his uniform shirt. I could

Barry Friedman

have put my fist in the hole which must have been made by the strafing Aussie. Pieces of gray lung tissue were evident in the depth of the wound but there was no movement of the lung, no sign of breathing. Blood seeped out of the wound, pooled on the deck. A holstered revolver was strapped to the airman's waist, and instinctively I reached to place my hand on it. I recall thinking that he might try to use it, although it took only a moment to realize that he wasn't ever going to reach for his pistol—or anything else. I placed my other hand on his neck and thought I felt a feeble carotid pulse. "He's still alive, barely." Blood began to seep from a corner of his mouth and when I again felt for a carotid pulse there was none. "He's dead."

I unstrapped the holstered revolver and tucked it in my belt. I turned and looked up into the grim faces of the crewmen who had formed a circle three deep around the body. Many had grown full beards, black and red and brown. Their slitted eyes stared down at the dead airman. Fierce, was the word that came to my mind. They didn't see a limp piece of lifeless flesh. They were looking at an enemy. An enemy who had tried to kill them, had succeeded killing others. An enemy who had strafed them and aimed torpedoes at them at Savo and at Tulagi and in the Gilbert Islands and Marshalls. They felt helpless then and had cowered in their battle stations, praying that this man's deadly missiles would not hit them. They had survived his attacks. Now they had him at their mercy. Never mind that

Survivor

his power to cause any more grief had poured out through the hole in his body. They were not to be denied vengeance.

I heard a ripping sound from behind and glanced around to see one of the crew tearing a part of the chute. Almost on signal, the others began slashing the silk parachute, some with knives, others rending it with their bare hands. They were like sharks in a feeding frenzy. They dragged the torn fragments through the blood that pooled around the body, waved the blood-soaked trophies around their heads, banners of triumph.

Barbaric? Isn't war itself barbaric? The man has left the cave but the cave remains in the man.

The years have dulled my memory of all the events that took place that day. I vaguely recall the body being wrapped in what remained of the parachute and being dumped into the sea. The act was impersonal. It symbolized the impersonality of warfare where adversaries are distant targets without faces, names, forms.

Later that day, a group of us sat around the wardroom table examining the contents of a small black wallet someone had taken from the airman's pocket. We spread out a few water-soaked papers covered with Japanese characters, probably letters from home. What I remember most vividly was a 2-inch square photograph of a smiling oriental woman. Wife? Mother? Sweetheart? I held it, stared at it and for a brief moment the enemy was not faceless.

Chapter 30

The radio shack of the *Russell* was a small room, barely large enough for two men and the radio equipment. On 6 June 1944, the room was packed shoulder-to-shoulder with crew members. Those who couldn't get into the room stood three deep outside listening to the crackling voice announcing that Allied troops had landed on the beaches of Normandy. Although the event was not unexpected, it provoked a loud cheer.

Another event that month was the awarding of a Purple Heart to Chief Quartermaster Robert Robinson for wounds he had incurred in October 1942 when his previous ship, *USS Meredith* was sunk by Japanese carrier-based planes off Guadalcanal. With the crew at attention, Captain Miller pinned the medal on Robbie's chest remarking that "This is the first Purple Heart awarded to a crewman on *Russell.*"

But the war was far from over on both sides of the world.

For the crew of *Russell,* the summer months of 1944 were spent escorting merchant ships carrying supplies up and down the New

Survivor

Guinea coast to ground forces, and ammunition and fuel to the warships. The Japanese made sporadic but ineffective air attacks on the ships in an effort to support their few remaining units in the New Guinea jungles.

Hollandia, in the approximate center of the 1600 mile north coast, was the main base of U.S. and Australian operations. It also provided a venue for recreation of a sort.

Supply ships had brought, in addition to food, beer which was distributed to the ships moored in Humboldt Bay, the harbor of Hollandia. Since consumption of alcoholic beverages were not permitted aboard ship, cans of beer were doled out to the liberty parties as they were going ashore.

Although there was nothing but beach, jungle and some partially cleared out fields at Hollandia, the crew members were happy to get their feet on solid ground if only for a few hours. It also gave them the opportunity to play baseball, to use the term loosely.

One of these ball games was memorable, if only for the wrong reason. It took place on a debris-filled "field," between a cemetery and a burned out ammunition dump.

Some of the *Russell's* "jocks" had found a baseball bat and misshapen softball that had been discarded by another ship's liberty party. The game was on—the engine room Black Gang vs the deck Swabbies.

On a regulation ball field Harrigan's dribbler would have been an easy out. On the dirt and weed patch, strewn with empty beer bottles, candy wrappers and debris, it went for a triple.

Next play he scored on a fielder's choice.

Harrigan rewarded himself with another bottle of beer from the ice-filled tub next to the bench. His third—maybe fourth, who's counting? After all, wasn't this R & R?

It was July 1944. July in New Guinea is a muggy month. So is March, April, May, June, and the other seven months. After Harrigan had scored, his team was twelve runs ahead—and there was only one out. The game was boring. Carrying his bottle of beer, he wandered to an adjacent field. If he had bothered to read the hand-printed notice posted on a tree, he would have learned he was in a restricted area. Further, he would have found out it was restricted because it contained bombs and shells, most of which had been detonated.

Harrigan strolled along, kicking a few empty shell cases. He stopped when he came to a large, gray, metallic object. He was a gunner's mate, first class, so he knew a 1000- pound bomb when he saw one. This one had its detonator. Not for long. Harrigan drained the last of his beer and tossed away the empty bottle. Carefully, he removed the detonator. He examined it for a few moments wondering what the inside of one of these things looked like. One way to find out. He took out his pocket knife and pried around the edge. This was going to be easy. The next moment, Harrigan was looking up at the sky. Lying on his back. He was sure he had been attacked by a

Survivor

swarm of bees.

The ballgame stopped when the players heard what sounded like a firecracker. Someone yelled, "Harrigan's there!"

The playing field emptied as the teams ran to see what had happened. They found Harrigan rubbing his hands over his blood-smeared face. Someone shouted, "Call the doc!"

When I got to him, Harrigan was still seated on the ground. Blood covered his face, neck and arms. I wiped away some of the blood from his face and saw that the skin was peppered with tiny black specks. Powder burns. They covered his neck, chest and upper arms. Miraculously, his eyes were spared.

His legs were shaky, but we got him to his feet and took him to an army first aid station a couple of hundred yards away. A medic and I got the blood cleared away and cleaned off as much of the gun powder as we could. We wrapped him in bandages and took him back to the ship.

For the next week, the Pharmacists' Mates and I cleaned and dressed his wounds. They were mostly superficial and, except for a slight amount of tattooing from the embedded gunpowder, there was little scarring.

A week later, we were back at sea. Harrigan was in sickbay having the last of his dressings removed. I stood back and examined him. "Harrigan, you're as pretty as you were before the explosion."

He surveyed his face in a mirror and started to leave. He

stopped, turned and said, "Hey, Doc, that was a Jap ammo dump, wasn't it?"

I shrugged. "I guess so. Why?

"Well, if I was wounded by enemy gunfire where's my Purple Heart?"

"Right there in your chest," I said. "Just above your Brown Liver and Red Spleen."

Chapter 31

In August 1944, Captain Miller was relieved as Commanding Officer of *Russell* and assigned to a larger ship. His replacement was Lieut. Commander John E. Wicks, USN, a native of Rutherford, New Jersey where, as his yearbook blurb states, "mosquitoes puncture tires." Captain Wicks, a Naval Academy graduate Class of 1938, was a six-foot, slim, sandy-haired man with a small mustache and a pleasant demeanor. In contrast to Captain Miller who distanced himself from the other officers, Wicks was "one of the boys." When the liberty detail went ashore at Hollandia, he joined the crew in a game of baseball, and proved to be very capable. Although not as authoritative as Miller, Wicks nevertheless demanded discipline in a way that earned for him the respect, admiration, and affection of all the ship's personnel.

Captain Wicks had two months to acquaint himself with his new command while ferrying convoys up and down the coast of New Guinea. Enemy planes that flew over the formations almost every day provided him the opportunity of observing the response of his crew to these attacks.

While *Russell* was fighting the war in the Southwest Pacific, a momentous event was taking place in Hawaii. President Franklin D. Roosevelt having just been nominated for an unprecedented fourth term, in July 1944 decided to call for a conference with General Douglas MacArthur, supreme commander of the South-West Pacific area, and Admiral Chester W. Nimitz, commander in chief of the U.S. Pacific Fleet. The purpose was to discuss how the fight against Japan should proceed.

Roosevelt arrived at Honolulu aboard the cruiser *Baltimore,* an hour after MacArthur had arrived after a 26-hour flight from Brisbane, Australia. Hardly settled in, MacArthur was summoned by Roosevelt to his cabin aboard ship. Always one for a symbolic gesture, MacArthur kept FDR and the top Pacific command waiting on the ship as he waved to the crowd and strutted to the top of the gangplank in an open shirt and leather jacket.

The following day, the meeting took place. Admiral Nimitz spoke first and argued to bypass the Philippines and attack Formosa. From there Japanese mainland could be bombed, and the supply of oil from the East Indies would be cut off.

Survivor

Then MacArthur stood to make his case in front of the maps laid out in front of the President. He reviewed his humiliation at Bataan and his dramatic announcement "I shall return." He stressed the importance to the morale of the American people of making the Philippines a high priority. Forget about Formosa, he argued. His plan, was to retake Manila. Now.

McArthur's argument was convincing and the President accepted his proposal. Further, he would expect Nimitz to assist MacArthur in the recapture of Luzon.

Although no official records of the conference exist, MacArthur privately told several people that he intimated to Roosevelt that it would make good politics for his coming election campaign, to show that the United States was making progress in the war against Japan.

The debate over whether to by-pass the Philippines and invade Formosa, continued in the Pentagon. The final decision to provide MacArthur his support came officially in mid-September after naval intelligence sources had revealed that the Japanese were most vulnerable at Leyte Island in the central Philippines.

Chapter 32

Now, after a year spent helping ground troops consolidate their position in New Guinea, *Russell* in company with dozens of other ships steamed northwest to the volcanic atoll of Ulithi, 850 miles from the Philippines. There they sortied with a fleet of more than 700 ships ranging in size from minesweepers to transports, battleships and aircraft carriers. When the assembled ships took off for the invasion of Leyte, it was the largest amphibious operation to date in the Pacific. The ocean from horizon-to-horizon was dotted with ships.

The Joint Chiefs of Staff designated General MacArthur supreme commander of sea, air, and land forces drawn from both the Southwest Pacific and Central Pacific theaters of operation. Ironically, MacArthur had been evacuated from Corregidor in a PT boat, now he was returning in the cruiser *Nashville.*

Allied naval forces for the Philippine campaign consisted primarily of the U.S. Seventh Fleet, commanded by Vice Adm. Thomas C. Kinkaid. Air support for the Leyte operation would be provided by the Seventh Fleet during the transport and amphibious phases, then transferred to Allied Air Forces, commanded by Lt. Gen. George C. Kenney, when conditions ashore allowed. More distant-covering air support would be provided by the four fast carrier task forces of Admiral Halsey's Third Fleet, whose operations would remain under overall command of Admiral Nimitz.

Although MacArthur was generally held in disdain by Navy personnel because of his excessive posturing, to his credit the planning of this operation was the work of a master. Every piece on this gigantic chessboard was accounted for and its mission was clearly defined. What could have been chaotic was orderly and well-organized.

The Philippine island of Leyte was to be the invasion site. Situated between Luzon to the north and Mindanao to the south, Leyte is one of the largest islnds of the Philippines. An estimate of the enemy's strength on Leyte as provided by Intelligence was that the Japanese had 20,000 troops on Leyte. The U.S. Commander, Lt. Gen. Walter Krueger, had over 200,000 ground troops at his disposal.

Preliminary operations for the Leyte invasion began at dawn on 17 October with minesweeping operations and the movement of the 6th Rangers toward three small islands in Leyte Gulf. The Rangers proceeded to erect navigation lights for the amphibious transports which would arrive three days later. Underwater demolition teams made sure the landing beaches for assault troops on Leyte were clear.

On 20 October, designated as A-Day when the invasion would begin, General Quarters on *Russell* was sounded at 0530 hrs and all hands hurried to their battle stations. As the ship entered Leyte Gulf, a lookout spotted a floating mine 150 yards to starboard. On the bridge, Captain Wicks passed the word to the flagship *Blue Ridge,* and a minesweep was dispatched to deal with it. An hour later, *Russell's* guns fired on an enemy bomber as it flew down the middle of the convoy, dropping its bomb about 150 feet from the ship's bow, rocking the ship but causing no structural damage. Although guns from every other ship in the area blasted anti-aircraft fire at the plane, it miraculously escaped only to be shot out of the sky by a Combat Air Patrol plane after it had cleared the convoy.

For the next four hours, the guns of the battleships, cruisers and destroyers raked the landing beaches at Tacloban. By the time the troops landed at 1000 hrs, any of the defenders who survived had retreated inland.

A wag aboard the *Russell* predicted that the first person to land on the beach would be a photographer walking backwards. True to his prophecy, when the Naval bombardment ceased, a landing craft moved close enough for General MacArthur to make a dramatic entrance wading through knee-deep surf. He announced to anyone in hearing distance, "People of the Philippines, I have returned! By the grace of Almighty God, our forces stand again on Philippine soil."

The *Russell's* crew was secured from General Quarters around noon that first day, but their brief period of rest was rudely interrupted when an enemy torpedo plane was observed coming directly at them. The plane was able to evade their firing with 5-inch/38 anti-aircraft guns, but was chased away by "friendlies" dispatched from one of the carriers before it could launch its torpedo.

With sporadic anti-aircraft fire coming from the beach and surrounding ships, the exhausted crew remained at their battle stations until night when the ship was darkened and lay-to in the Leyte Gulf off shore from Tacloban where the troops had landed.

A historic day—but there were more to come.

Chapter 33

Although the landing of Allied troops at Tacloban was carried out as planned, it was a given that further progress by the invading troops would be made as difficult as possible by the Japanese. So it was no surprise when Captain Wicks received word from Vice Admiral Daniel Barbey who commanded the task group to which *Russell* had been assigned, that as many as 10,000 enemy troops were poised to cross the San Juanico Strait, a narrow channel between Samar Island just to the north, and Leyte. Obviously, the Japanese planned to attack the American troops from their rear, and destroy the ammunition and supplies they had transported to the beachhead. The attack, as Naval Intelligence had learned was to take place under cover of darkness on 22 October, two days after the Tacloban landing. *Russell* was dispatched to the site where the enemy troops would be infiltrating.

On shore, a coast watcher observed Japanese troops massing to cross the Strait. It has never been revealed whether the coast watcher was an American or a Filipino but he was in radio contact with the

Survivor

Russell. At 2005 hrs on the night of 22 October the observer, nicknamed Foxhole Charlie by the *Russell* crew, began transmitting target areas. For the next fifteen minutes, the *Russell's* main battery fired at the shore target, making corrections as directed by the spotter. The infiltrators were temporarily driven back, but an hour later the spotter radioed that they had resumed their advance. *Russell* gunners illuminated the area with a star shell, and blasted away continuously for a half hour. Intermittently through the night, the guns roared at targets, periodically firing star shells, as designated by the shore spotter. At daybreak, the transmissions suddenly stopped. Apparently Foxhole Charlie either had been located and disposed of by the enemy, or he had vectored gunfire on to his own position and had been wiped out by "friendly" fire. But his mission had been accomplished. The counterattack never materialized. *Russell* had expended 400 rounds of 5"/38 shells and 27 star shells in thwarting the assault.

The *Russell's* night of gunfire came with a cost. The aft steering station, the gyro repeater and the rudder angle indicator were all damaged. Fortunately, the damage did not prevent the ship from taking part in the rest of the battle at Leyte Gulf. Although the supply of 5"/38 armament was rapidly becoming depleted, *Russell* still had enough ammunition the afternoon of 23 October and the following day, to repel a series of attacks by enemy bombers. By now, the ship was relying more on her 20 mm and 40 mm guns for firepower.

In spite of the anti-aircraft fire by *Russell* and other ships of the task force that accounted for shooting down seven of the attacking planes, some of the others got through to bomb and seriously damage a Liberty supply ship and sink a troop-carrying LST. The latter, was set afire by an enemy plane that crashed into its deck. The ship may have been one of the first victims of a Kamikaze attack. In the days that followed, attacks by suicidal pilots became much more frequent, an indication that the Japanese had become desperate.

During a lull in the action, a native dugout with outriggers on either side, manned by half a dozen Filipinos, pulled alongside *Russell*. In the dugout sat their prisoner, a naked and bloodied Japanese, his hands bound behind him. In fairly good English, one of the natives explained that the prisoner had been caught raping a young Filipina. They had castrated him and wanted the *Russell* to take him on board and hang him.

Captain Wicks was not about to burden the ship with a prisoner when the crew was busy fighting off air attacks. He certainly was not going to play executioner. While he was in sympathy with the Filipinos, rather than just dismiss the group and tell them to do their own hanging, he called Admiral Barbey on the ship-to-ship radio for his advice.

One could picture a sly grin on the Admiral's face when he told Captain Wicks, "Point them in the direction of General MacArthur's

Survivor

LST. Philippine President Sergio Osmena is there with him. It'll be a good opportunity for him to exercise his presidential power."

The prisoner and his captors were last seen headed for MacArthur's flagship.

On 24 October the aircraft carrier *Princeton* was patrolling off the east coast of Luzon. Its planes were bombing Clark Field to prevent Japanese planes from attacking the troops establishing a beachhead on Leyte, 330 nautical miles to the south.

At 0930 hrs. a single Judy, bomber, was sighted by *Princeton's* lookouts, diving on their vessel. The Judy dropped two bombs. One missed and fell harmlessly into the sea. The other 550-pound bomb fell almost in the center of *Princeton's* deck. Fire broke out smoke enveloped the ship.

The cruiser *Birmingham* came alongside to help fight the fire. Harry Popham, aboard *Birmingham*, watched from the bridge while the firefighting detail played hoses on the *Princeton's* deck. The following are excerpts from his eyewitness account entitled "Eyewitness to Tragedy: Death of USS Princeton" in the May 1997 online issue of *Weider's "Historynet.com."*

"We saw a single tongue of flame shoot out from the area of the after elevator, followed by an enormous puff of white smoke like a billowy cumulus cloud. To our horror, a slender column of pale orange-colored smoke shot several hundred feet straight up. All hell broke loose with an enormous eruption. One hundred and thirty feet of *Princeton's* stern blew off, as well as 180 feet of her flight deck.

"The force of the shock wave tumbled me backward 30 or 40 feet and about 10 feet into the air before dropping me on the deck. The shock wave hit me a split second before the thunder of the explosion reached my ears. I was stunned momentarily, yet at the same time my senses were heightened. When the roar of the explosion abated, I became aware of burning hot shrapnel raining down all around me. The shrapnel was burning through my clothes in what seemed to be hundreds of places. I had to get out from under that shower of hot steel. When I glanced down I saw that my right knee was mangled, so I thought I would get up on my left leg and hop to the overhanging No. 4 turret. But my left leg would not support me because it was broken. I tried to crawl on my belly, but the pea-sized, gravel-like bits of *Princeton* on the deck painfully burned my hands and forearms as well as the nape of my neck. All I could do was roll around on the deck, trying to escape the searing pain. Finally, the shrapnel stopped falling and the pieces of steel cooled. I collected myself enough to look around at hundreds of dead or unconscious bodies. Out of maybe 300 crew members on the after starboard deck of *Birmingham*, there was only one person other than myself who was conscious.

Survivor

"On my back and propped on my elbows, I surveyed the extent of the damage. Wherever I looked there was carnage. Rivers of blood poured from the scuppers into the sea. It was a scene from a nightmare. I was wondering what to do when another shipmate, John Miksis, suddenly appeared from nowhere. His face was burned cork black, and he was completely covered with soot. At first I did not recognize him. Only his voice identified him to me. Miksis promised to find some more help and went below. While I waited for John's return, my limited view was of the deck strewn with assorted body parts and rivers of blood draining into the water.

"Aboard *Princeton*, four people had miraculously escaped the incredible explosion that had originated abaft the after elevator on the hangar deck. They were about 280 to 300 feet from the origin of the explosion. One of them, Gene Mitchell, sustained multiple wounds. Mitchell pulled himself together enough to look over at *Birmingham*. What he saw was so ghastly and traumatic that he experienced flashbacks for years. He saw the same horrors and rivers of blood washing the deck as I had.

"*Princeton's* skipper grudgingly gave orders to his damage-control party to abandon ship The gallant light carrier was to be scuttled by torpedoes."

Birmingham had suffered major damage and limped back to Mare Island, California for repairs.

The night and day of 24-25 October 1944 is remarkable for its complexity. The Allied Naval forces in the Leyte engagement were divided between the Third Fleet commanded by Vice Admiral William Halsey, and the Seventh Fleet headed by Vice Admiral Thomas Kinkaid. Halsey's fleet came under Admiral Nimitz' Central Pacific Command, while the Seventh Fleet was responsible to General MacArthur, Commander of the Southwest Pacific Forces.

The landing forces were supported by the Seventh Fleet, while Halsey's job was to protect and support Kinkaid's ships.

The Japanese committed practically all their ships to the Leyte Campaign. They divided their fleet into three prongs. One group would steam through the Surigao Strait, south of Leyte, a second group would approach through the San Bernadino Strait and proceed south to Tacloban where the Allied ground forces were establishing their beachhead. This was the largest and most powerful of the Japanese Naval units. It included two superbattleships, the *Yamato* and the *Musashi* which would blast and decimate the Allied landing force.

The third Japanese Naval force would sail north of Leyte. It was a decoy consisting of four aircraft carriers which carried no planes.

Survivor

Its purpose was to lure the U.S. warships away from the troop transports in the Leyte Gulf, leaving them unprotected.

Halsey swallowed the bait. His scout planes located the decoy carriers to the north, and considering them to be the main threat, his Third Fleet with three U.S. fast carrier groups and six battleships raced north. The San Bernadino Strait was left unguarded. To make matters worse, he had not informed Kinkaid he was going north. *Russell* and another destroyer, Lang, were dispatched to guard the entrance to the Surigao Strait. Their orders were to prevent any enemy battleships from breaking through. Quite a feat since *Russell* was down to its last 15 five-inch ammo. The only other armament beside the 20 mm and 40mm popguns, were torpedoes.

At 0245, from the deck of *Russell* observers could see down the Surigao Strait flashes of light and hear the thunder of gunfire. The enemy was approaching. At the same time, came a radio report that the Japanese ships were being engaged in the Surigao Strait by the first line of defense, Motor Torpedo Boats, and the second battle line consisting of destroyers, cruisers and old, slow battleships. The smaller craft fired their torpedoes at the Japanese warships, then raced back toward *Russell* leaving the big boys to carry on the fight. By now, the ships and flame from the muzzles of their big guns were in sight of *Russell.* Intermittent explosions and bright flashes marked hits on the Japanese ships. The pyrotechnics in the darkness of that night would have put to shame the most dazzling of Fourth of July displays. If it weren't so frightening it would have been entrancing.

Meanwhile, early the morning of 25 October, a few miles north of Surigao Strait the enemy's Central Force of superbattleships had broken through to the San Bernadino Strait and were attacking the small unarmed escort carrier groups whose call signals were "Taffy One, Two and Three." This action was taking place off the east coast of Samar, the island just north of Leyte.

Admiral Kinkaid put in a desperate call for help in plain language to Admiral Halsey who he thought was guarding the entrance to San Bernadino Strait, but instead was chasing shadows in the form of carriers without planes, far north. Halsey ignored the request for nearly three hours.

Every available destroyer was ordered to guard the entrance to the Leyte Gulf and at all costs prevent the enemy from getting to the troops that had just established a beachhead at Tacloban, at the west end of the Leyte Gulf.

Russell had been guarding the Surigao Strait entrance, but when the enemy ships came under attack by 28 Motor Torpedo Boats, 28 destroyers, 8 cruisers and 6 old battleships, the Japanese withdrew. Only one of the Japanese ships, a destroyer, survived. *Russell's* services were now needed in the battle that was shaping up in the Leyte Gulf, just off the coast of Samar.

Admiral Barby called over to *Russell.* "Pony Boy (*Russell's* call signal) you are released from your station here. Saddle up and join the other DDs (destroyers)."

Lieut. Bill Bargeloh, the Executive Officer, took the message and radioed back, "This is Pony Boy. We're saddled up and riding east to meet the Rising Sun."(The Japanese flag depicts the rising sun)

Barbey replied, "Good luck, Pony Boy, and good hunting!"

At flank speed, *Russell* dashed to join four other destroyers lined up to block the east entrance to the Leyte Gulf.

Another message from Admiral Barby: "At all costs, enemy superbattleship *Yamoto* and her group must not get inside (Leyte Gulf) to attack transports and landing."

At the west end of the Gulf, a similar blockade was formed by three destroyers of the Taffy Three unit: *Johnston, Hoel,* and *Heermann,* and four DEs (Destroyer Escorts), *Dennis, John C. Butler, Raymond,* and *Samuel B.Roberts.* In addition, Taffy Three had six small escort carriers, but they were slow and had very little armament.

Barry Friedman

At about 0700 hrs, the Japanese superbattleship *Yamoto,* having broken through the San Bernadino Strait, came upon Taffy Three by surprise. From 23 miles away, the guns of the big battleship and her accompanying cruisers began straddling the escort carriers with shell fire. The U.S. destroyers tried to protect them by laying down a smoke screen as the jeep carriers tried to scramble out of range, but one, *Gambier Bay* was hit with several high explosive shells and sank. A second escort carrier, *St.Lo* caught another volley and was finished off by a Kamikaze plane that crashed on her flight deck. Two others took hits but managed to stay afloat. Only two were unscathed.

While all this was going on, the U.S. destroyers and DEs were running into a buzz saw. They began the impossible task of attacking the battleships and cruisers with torpedoes.

Taffy Three's battle is described in detail by James D. Hornfischer in his excellent book, *The Last Stand of the Tin Can Sailors.* To attempt to do other than summarize it, does it an injustice.

Although the destroyers and DEs scored hits on several of the enemy ships, the mission, heroic though it was, proved suicidal and resulted in the sinking of *Hoel, Johnston,* and *Samuel B. Roberts.* Even the Japanese were impressed by the tenaciousness of the U.S. sailors. One of the *Johnston* survivors reported that while he and a number of others from his ship were afloat in the water one of the

Survivor

enemy ships cruised by, their crew lining the rails in tribute to their gallantry.

Although crippled and in some cases mortally wounded, the ships and planes of Taffy Three managed to inflict damage on the enemy sinking three heavy cruisers and damaging several other ships.

But on the verge of annihilating Taffy Three, inexplicably the Japanese ships reversed course and retreated through the San Bernadino Strait.

Admiral Clifton Sprague recalled:

"I could not believe my eyes, but it looked as if the whole Japanese fleet was indeed retiring. However, it took a whole series of reports from circling planes to convince me. And still I could not get the fact to soak into my battle-numbed brain. At best, I had expected to be swimming by this time."

While the Battle of Samar was raging, Vice Admiral Thomas Kinkaid was sending a series of desperate calls for help from Halsey's Task Force 34 which was well north of the action:

"My situation is critical."

"Fast battleships are urgently needed immediately at Leyte Gulf."

"Need fast battleships and air support."

In fleet headquarters at Pearl Harbor, Admiral Chester Nimitz had been monitoring Kinkaid's calls and sent Halsey a message which his radioman recorded as: "Turkey trots to water where is TF 34 the world wonders."

It was customary to encrypt the vital parts of radioed messages with gibberish at the beginning and end. Thus, the prefix, "Turkey trots to water," and the suffix, "the world wonders," were not meant to be parts of the *real* message which was, "Where is TF 34?"

The radioman who recorded the message, for some reason removed the prefix but left the suffix, so it was handed to Halsey as "Where is TF34-the world wonders."

That Halsey was infuriated, understates by several orders of magnitude, his reaction. Nevertheless, he turned his ships around and charged toward Leyte Gulf, but by the time he arrived the action was over and the damage had been done.

When historians sort out the various segments of the Battle of Leyte Gulf which include the battles of Surigao Strait and Samar, they place the pieces in proper order. But, except for a few who saw the whole picture from their command posts, those who lived in the sound and fury of battle saw only their small corner of the war. It was utter confusion.

From the deck of the *Russell,* as we listened to the roar of guns, watched the distant flashes of light, and heard the incessant, seemingly senseless chatter coming through the radio, all we could be sure of was that it was a hell of a battle. In the idiom of the day, one word

Survivor

sums it up: SNAFU, the acronym for Situation Normal-All Fucked Up.

Obviously the enemy was as confused as well. The Japanese Admiral-turned-quarterback who metaphor-ically had the ball on his opponent's one-yard line, first down and goal to go, turned around and walked off the field forfeiting the game.

Chapter 34

Lieut.(jg) Joe Logan was first in line at morning sick call one day in early November 1944. He complained of a persistent cough, present for about three or four weeks. In retrospect, I recalled he coughed frequently during meals in the wardroom.

Joe was about twenty-six-years old, a handsome, sandy-haired man who spoke with a Mississippi drawl. When we attended USO dances in Honolulu the girls went glassy-eyed over him.

"I thought I ought to see what you can do for this damned cough," he said. Then as an afterthought, "Last few days I noticed some blood in my sputum."

Alarm bells went off in my head. Bloody sputum in a young man ? TB?

"Have you lost any weight?"

He shrugged. "Maybe. My pants seem looser than they were a few months ago."

His temperature was 99.8 degrees Fahrenheit. Slightly elevated.

"Night sweats? Are your pajamas soaked with perspiration?"

Joe chuckled. "We're in New Guinea, remember. This place is more humid than back home in Mississippi."

"Do you get tired more easily than you used to?"

"Come on, Doc. We're at General Quarters morning and night. Sure I get tired."

I put my stethoscope to his chest. At the upper part of his right thorax his breath sounds were abnormal.

He coughed into his fist. A dry cough. I gave him a paper cup and asked him to bring up some sputum. Tinged with pink.

Short of being torpedoed or bombed, nothing strikes more fear into medical personnel aboard ship than someone with a communicable disease. In 1944, tuberculosis ranked as the sixth leading cause of death in the U.S. Direct exposure to sputum droplets coughed up from an individual with pulmonary tuberculosis could easily cause the infection to spread to others. And the 300 men confined to the relatively close quarters aboard ship were at risk. Further, there was the possibility that other members of the crew were also infected multiplying the possibility of spread. I wanted to isolate Logan as best I could until I knew what I was dealing with.

Logan said, "Probably a cigarette cough, right Doc?"

"Joe," I said, "I want you to go back to your cabin and get in bed."

He held up a hand. "Whoa, Doc. I've got the 1200 o'clock watch. I'll go after I get off watch at 1600."

"Forget the watch. I'll get someone to take it for you."

He protested. "But I'm not sick."

"You've got a cough and fever. In my book you're not well. I don't want you spreading whatever you've got to anyone else."

He started to argue, but I was firm and he reluctantly agreed.

Before alarming Joe or anyone else, I had to make sure of the diagnosis. A chest X-Ray would have been a big help, but only the large ships had X-Ray equipment. However, my Chief Pharmacist's Mate had been trained as a laboratory technician. I explained the problem to him and gave him the cup containing the sputum and asked him to do an acid-fast stain. This is a test where a sample of a tuberculous secretion or tissue is placed on a microscope slide and stained with a reagent which would show the presence of tubercle bacilli as tiny red rods. It was a long shot since more than 10,000 organisms per ml of sputum are needed to visualize the bacilli with a high power microscope lens. Usually a cup of centrifuged sputum is necessary to concentrate these little red bugs. And our single eyepiece microscope was vintage von Leeuwenhoek. But it was worth a try.

At the time, we were screening a convoy of LSTs down the New Guinea coast. We would be pulling into Hollandia later that day. To isolate him from the rest of the crew as well as have the necessary tests performed, I planned to take him to the base hospital there as soon as we made port.

Survivor

After seeing that Joe was settled in his bunk, I went to the bridge and told the Captain my suspicion. He agreed and radioed ahead to have a jeep meet us when we docked.

As we pulled into Humboldt Bay, the harbor of Hollandia, the Chief Pharmacist's Mate reported that the stain hadn't shown any tubercle bacilli which did not surprise me because of the small sample. But TB was still my presumptive diagnosis.

A jeep with a driver waited at the foot of the gangway. Joe and I piled in and we drove in silence to the 27th General Hospital that had just been set up by the Army. Although it was mostly a series of tents in which patients lay in cots, the surgical and X-Ray units were constructed of wood and were well-equipped.

I waited while a technician took Joe's X-Ray and developed it. I sat next to the radiologist while he put the X-Ray film, still wet, on a view box. The radiologist pointed to an area at the upper right lobe of Joe's lung. "That's a small cavity."

Although a more complete microscopic examination of his sputum would be necessary to confirm the diagnosis, there was little question; Joe had cavitary TB. The risk of spread of infection to non-infected persons from individuals with cavitary tuberculosis is very high.

I arranged to have him admitted to the hospital and while we waited I gave him the unpleasant news.

Barry Friedman

Before the advent of streptomycin and other anti-tuberculosis medications which came about a few years later, to many people the diagnosis of tuberculosis was a death sentence. The fact was that with rest, proper nutrition and the occasional need for minor surgical procedures, the disease could usually be arrested—we never referred to it as "cured" because the relapse rate was substantial.

Joe was understandably shaken, but I assured him that with treatment he'd get well and would be able to lead a normal life. He'd be evacuated back to the States where further treatment would be carried out in a Naval Hospital. His service in the Navy was over, of course, but it was more important that he get well.

Before I left the hospital, I had the supply officer fill a box with vials of tuberculin PPD (purified protein derivative), tuberculin syringes and needles. I'd have to screen the crew for evidence of the disease by injecting a tiny amount of the tuberculin between the skin layers. If active tuberculosis was present, a raised area of induration measuring 10 mm or more would appear at the site of injection in 48 to 72 hours.

For most of the following day, the crew lined up while the Pharmacist's Mates and I injected tuberculin into the skin of their forearms. There was plenty of grumbling about the cancelled liberty, but I wanted the men to remain aboard ship until I was able to determine if anyone else had contracted the disease.

Survivor

As it turned out, one of the engine room men had a definite positive reaction and in three other crew men the reaction was questionable. On questioning, the man who tested positive admitted that he had been coughing, but was sure it was from smoking two packs of cigarettes a day so he didn't bother to report to sickbay. I took the four to the base hospital where X-Rays showed evidence of tuberculosis in the man with the positive reaction, and he was admitted to the hospital. The other three were free of disease in their lungs. It was possible that they harbored the disease in another organ such as the kidney or bone, but unlikely since it would have metastasized to these other sites from a primary pulmonary source.

The Naval Battle of Leyte Gulf was now history, and the ground forces on the island were mopping up the pockets of resistance. But the Battle of the Philippines was far from over.

For two months, *Russell* shuttled between Leyte and Hollandia, New Guinea escorting merchant ships and LSTs carrying supplies to the ground forces. Frequent air attacks on the convoys from planes based on Luzon kept *Russell's* gunners busy. Evidence of the enemy's desperation was the increasing frequency of Kamikaze suicide attacks. As we learned after the war, commanders of the Japanese Airforce noted that the most effective way to inflict damage upon Allied warships was to crash planes into them. One crash could do more damage than 10 planes firing machine guns. It was decided then that pilots would purposely crash their bomb-loaded planes into American warships.

Generally, Kamikaze pilots were university students motivated by obligation, and loyalty to family and country. A typical pilot was a student in his twenties. He prepared for his fiery destiny by writing farewell letters and poems to loved ones, receiving a "thousand-stitch sash," and by holding a ceremony — a drink of water that gave him a "spiritual lifting" before wedging himself between 550-pound bombs.

They adamantly believed that they were fighting for their Emperor God. Following the call for Kamikaze pilots three times as many applied for suicide flights as the number of planes available. Experienced pilots were turned down. They were needed to train the younger men how to fly to their deaths.

During November and December 1944, in the convoys screened by *Russell,* Kamikazes were responsible for the sinking of a merchant vessel and two LSTs.

In late November, an incident occurred on board that troubled the entire crew. While squabbles among young men confined together for long periods at sea is not unusual, they are quickly and painlessly resolved. But during General Quarters one day James Wheeler, a Seaman 1/C struck Lieut. Bob Stuart, the Gunnery Officer. Striking a superior officer automatically calls for a General Court Martial.

At the preliminary hearing, one of the man who'd witnessed the affair testified that Wheeler had done something that irritated Lieut.

Survivor

Stuart. He berated Wheeler "using vulgar and personally derogatory language. Wheeler lost control, and when Lieut. Stuart got right up in his face and called him a derogatory name Wheeler struck him."

The Court-Martial found the young sailor guilty. He was detached from the ship and sent to Naval Prison at Mare Island, California. Stuart received a letter of reprimand and was also detached from *Russell.* He was an Annapolis graduate, one of only three regular Navy officers aboard ship, the rest were Naval Reserve on active duty. The incident probably cost him any chance of promotion and in effect ended his further career in the Navy.

In mid-December, one of the merchant ships in *Russell's* convoy signaled that they needed the services of a doctor. As the only doctor in the convoy, I was elected. In order to bring the proper equipment, I asked the signalman to find out what the problem was.

The reply: "Sore throat."

Captain Wicks and I exchanged puzzled looks. "They need a doctor for a sore throat?"

I was about to send a message telling the patient to gargle with salt water, when the merchant ship clarified: "Can't swallow. Hardly breathe. Hurry!"

While the Captain brought the ship as close as possible alongside the merchant vessel, I ran down to sickbay, tossed an airway and a few instruments, needles and syringes into my kit and hurried back on deck.

Barry Friedman

The deck crew had already strung a line between the two ships and I was strapped into a Boatswain's Chair to be hauled across. A Boatswain's Chair consists of a piece of wood to serve as a seat, suspended by ropes which are attached to the overhead line strung between two ships. Although I had watched the transfer of a number of men, mostly airmen who'd been rescued when their planes crashed and were being returned to their carrier, it's a little different when you're the one being hung out to dry across 30 yards of ocean. The water beneath you seems to be rushing like a mountain stream after a winter runoff even though the ships were cruising at only about five knots. I gulped a few times when the line went a little slack and I had to yank up my feet to keep them out of the water.

Once I'd been pulled on to the merchant ship's deck, the First Mate told me that the patient was the ship's skipper. He'd been well until yesterday when he'd had a very sore throat, increasing difficulty swallowing, and now he "looked like he was choking to death."

We hurried to the Captain's cabin and found him, a man who appeared to be in his late forties, clutching his throat and taking short sonorous breaths. His face was bluish and his forehead burned with fever. He pointed to his mouth. I asked him to open his mouth and with great difficulty he was able to open it about half an inch. I wedged couple of a tongue depressors on edge between his teeth and I managed to get it open enough to see his pharynx. The problem was immediately apparent: a peritonsillar abscess the size of a ping pong ball was obstructing his airway. Fortunately, I had packed in my kit a large syringe and some large bore needles. He was in desperate straits, so I didn't want to take the time to inject a local anesthetic.

"This may hurt a little," I said.

He nodded and motioned for me to do whatever I had to.

I plunged the needle into the abscess and drew thick pus into the syringe. With the abscess collapsed like a deflated balloon, he drew in several deep breaths. His color immediately turned a bright pink.

He grabbed my hand and in a hoarse whisper said, "Thanks. You saved my life."

I shrugged an "aw-shucks."

These were the days before penicillin so I instructed him to gargle every few hours to irrigate his pharynx, and to have his tonsils removed when he could get to a medical facility.

Back on deck from my "house call," the merchant ship's crew had already sent my fee—a gallon of ice cream—to the *Russell*.

My trip back in the Boatswain's Chair turned out to be an adventure. When I was halfway across, the *Russell* crew, a playful bunch, had great sport putting slack on the line until I was barely out of the water. I could hear them chant, "Dunk the Doc. Dunk..."until Captain Wicks leaned over the bridge wing and yelled for them to "knock it off!"

Chapter 35

Nineteen-forty-five. A new year, a new mission for *Russell:* Allied forces were poised to return to Luzon three years after the island, along with the rest of the Philippines, had been taken over by the Japanese.

Luzon is the largest island of the Philippines and the home of the country's capital, Manila.

On 5 January, *Russell* as part of a huge task force, steamed 300 miles north of Leyte to the west coast of Luzon. The Japanese, having lost most of her naval and air power was now resorting to suicide missions in a desperate attempt to keep the Allies from inching nearer to the Japanese homeland. In addition to Kamikaze attacks, the convoy was plagued by suicide swimmers and small boats. The swimmers, termed *Fukuryu* ("Crouching dragons") attacked in darkness. Each swimmer was armed with a mine containing 33 pounds of explosive fitted to a 16-foot bamboo pole. They would dive beneath a slowly moving ship and stick the pole into its hull. The ex-

Survivor

plosion damaged or destroyed the ship destroying themselves in the process.

The *Shinyo* ("Sea Quake") were Japanese suicide boats. These fast wooden motorboats were driven by one man, to speeds of around 30 knots/h. They were typically equipped with two depth charges fitted in the bow of the boat. The driver would ram the boat into the hull of a ship and the resulting explosion would kill the driver and cause considerable damage to the ship.

As *Russell* passed the many small islands en route to the invasion site at Lingayan Gulf, about 60 miles north of Manila, radar picked up numerous blips representing fleets of suicide boats, "skunks" in radar terminology, lurking along the shores. While none attacked *Russell,* they did sink two gunboats and damaged six Landing Craft Support vessels (LCS.)

On the night of 7 January as the convoy was approaching the entrance to Manila Bay, radar picked up an unidentified target that at first appeared to be two ships at a distance of 11 miles. As the target grew closer, a star shell fired by *Russell* illuminated what now could be identified as a Japanese destroyer exiting the bay. *Russell* commenced firing, the first salvo hitting the enemy ship's after superstructure. The firing was joined by three other destroyers, *USS Charles Ausburne (DD-570)*, *USS Braine (DD-630)*, and *USS Shaw (DD-373.)* It was like shooting a fish in a barrel. Although flashes of gunfire could be seen coming from the guns of the Japanese vessel, none of the U.S. ships were hit.

Russell's guns were on rapid fire 2300 yards from the target. By the illumination of star shells, the enemy vessel could be seen listing, then suddenly a violent explosion sent flames shooting high in the night sky, probably the magazine had been hit and the ship sank quickly. After the war, records revealed that the Japanese ship was the destroyer *Hinoki* and was lost with all hands.

From Rear Admiral Barby's flagship *Russell* received a TBS call, "Well done. Good shooting. Search area and pick up survivors."

At the direction of Lieut. Skahill, the Executive Officer, Ensign Robert Robinson went aft with a Thompson machine gun looking for survivors as *Russell* stopped. Cries could be heard, but the several men in the water swam away and were lost in the darkness. They refused to be rescued.

For Robby Robinson, it was a moment filled with irony. In October 1942 he had been Chief Quartermaster on *USS Meredith*, a destroyer, when it was sunk off Guadalcanal by Japanese carrier-based planes. While he and a handful of survivors were helplessly wallowing in the water, they were strafed by Japanese planes. Now, he and his *Russell* shipmates were "risking their lives to a submarine attack, by stopping the ship and entreating the surviving Japanese sailors to swim closer to the ship so they could be rescued. The contrast was a direct reflection of two very different philosophies of life. (I) realized

Survivor

that I hated the helpless survivors less than I hated their philosophy of life."

The invading force reached Lingayan Gulf early on the morning of 9 January. For three days prior to the landing, a heavy naval and air bombardment of suspected Japanese defenses on Lingayen had been carried out. Underwater demolition teams found no beach obstacles, and encountered sparse opposing forces. Aircraft and naval artillery bombardment of the landing areas was also carried out in spite of frequent Kamikaze attacks.

At 0930 on 9 January about 68,000 men under General Walter Krueger of the U.S. 6th Army landed at the coast of Lingayen Gulf meeting no opposition. Landings continued over the next few days while *Russell* lay off shore screening the transport *Warren.*

On 11 January I stood on a wing of the bridge alongside the officer who had the conn early that morning. If you were with the liberating forces, the sight was awesome. If you were the enemy, it must have been frightening. As far as you could see on the horizon, were ships. Ships of all sizes and description.

Russell lay about 4,000 yards off the landing area designated Beach White 2. We watched as troops of the Army 25th Division were off-loaded from the *Warren* to the LCVPs, blunt-nosed landing craft which would take them to the beach. The shoreline had been raked by our aircraft, so radio messages crackling over the TBS on the bridge told us that the landings were virtually unopposed.

We scanned the skies for Kamikazes, the suicide planes that had swooped in at low level almost daily, causing considerable damage to our ships. But none were flying today.

At 1000 hours an excited voice over the bridge radio informed us that one of the landing craft mistakenly had landed on a section of beach that had not been cleared of enemy. The soldiers aboard the craft waded ashore where they were blasted by machine gun fire, mortar and three-inch shells. In moments, the water was littered with torn bodies. Some wounded survivors tried to swim out to sea, others scurried back into the LCVP which was now aground, unable to budge. The defenseless landing craft now became a sitting duck target for enemy mortar shells, one of which hit the engine house. The explosion sent fragments of metal and wood flying into the army troops and navy crewmen killing or wounding several more. They tried to fight back with the few weapons that had not been lost, but when it was obvious they had no chance, they leaped out of the boat and tried to swim away under constant fire by the Japanese defenders.

Another landing craft saw the attack and radioed frantically for help. Captain Wicks ordered the ship's motor whaleboat to be lowered into the water to pick up survivors.

Survivor

He saw me on the bridge. "Doc, they're going to need medical assistance. Better go with them and take a Pharmacist's Mate along."

I hurried down to the deck where the motor whaleboat was swinging in its davits. One of the Pharmacist's Mates and I clambered into it as it was being lowered. I had with me the small canvas sack with first aid equipment I carried when we were at General Quarters.

The small boat pulled away from *Russell* pitching wildly through the choppy waters as we headed toward the beach. A spotter plane circling overhead directed us to a group of about twenty men dog-paddling in the water about 500 yards from shore. We pulled alongside and started hauling them into our boat while mortar shells splashed to either side of us, vectoring closer and closer. Even now, more than sixty-five years later, I can recall the helpless feeling I had as I waited for the hit that seemed inevitable. Suddenly, one of our planes dove at the beach, raking the enemy guns. The mortar fire stopped and I felt as though I'd been given another life. Soon, another rescue boat joined us pulling in as many of the men we could find floundering in the sea. We started back to the *Russell* with a dozen survivors in our boat, most of whom had been wounded. In the pitching and yawing motor whaleboat, all we could do for them was administer morphine and put large gauze pressure dressings on their bleeding wounds.

Barry Friedman

When we finally pulled alongside the *Russell*, I felt like a lost child that had found its mother. The motor whaleboat was raised to deck level, crewmen already had lined up litters on the deck, and we transferred the men to the wardroom, the triage area.

Most of the wounds were to the arms and legs. Anyone with a penetrating abdominal wound would not have been able to swim away from the shore and would already have drowned or lay dead on the beach. One of the survivors had a small puncture wound in his chest through which air hissed as he breathed. I taped a compression dressing over it plugging the hole Two of the men had mutilated hands, their fingers either missing or dangling by threads of tissue. I recall snipping off the remnants of their fingers like you'd trim dead leaves from a plant. I marveled that they were able to paddle out from the beach with their mangled hands. Unquestionably, the adrenalin pumping through their bodies gave them the power to perform feats that would have been physically impossible under ordinary circumstances.

While I was applying a dressing to the partially amputated hand of one of the men, from the edge of my vision I spotted a man with the large sliver of wood in his neck. In the commotion of the rescue operation, I hadn't noticed his injury. Now he was seated on the wardroom bench murmuring softly, barely moving his lips as though fearful of disturbing the object piercing his throat. "Get this friggin' thing out, please."

Survivor

I inspected it more closely. The end of the wood protruded about four inches out of the skin, two inches to the left of his Adam's apple. The visible part of the wood measured about an inch and a half in width and half an inch in thickness. It had been driven so deeply into the tissue of his throat that the skin over the back of his neck was tented by the other end of the stick. When I gently wiggled the end that protruded, the other end moved under the skin at the back of his neck, so I knew it was one long piece.

I had seen some weird injuries but nothing to prepare me for this. Was the stick plugging a vital structure like the carotid artery or the jugular vein? If I removed it would it be like uncorking a bottle of champagne? My mind drew anatomic cross-sections of the neck. In addition to the large blood vessels there were some important nerves, a windpipe and esophagus to concern me. I reflected that I could leave it in and wait until he was transferred to a ship that had an operating room. There it could be extracted with instruments and hands necessary to handle a sudden gush of blood, if that should happen.

I asked one of the Pharmacist's Mates to get some idea from the Captain when the men could be transferred. Meanwhile, I had the other Pharmacist's Mates get the sterile surgical pack. It contained enough instruments to perform most simple operations.

The first Pharmacist's Mate was back. "The Captain doesn't know when we can transfer the men."

Barry Friedman

The young man with the neck wound was pleading. "Please. please, get it out."

I stood peering down at him, thinking, debating, finally reasoning that if the carotid artery had been pierced, he probably would have already bled out. The jugular vein might be caught by the wood fragment. But I recalled that the few times as an intern I'd done jugular vein punctures, trying to spear the vein, even with a sharp needle, was no easy matter. The wall of the vein was thick, would roll away from the tip of the needle. The chances of it being punctured by the wood fragment were slim—I hoped.

Finally, I made up my mind. "Let's do it."

Behind me I could hear murmurs from the crowd of observers, other officers, some of the crew. I felt like a matador climbing into a bullring.

I pulled on a fresh pair of sterile rubber gloves. I'm sure this was more to bide time rather than for sterility. After all, the wood wasn't sterile; it hadn't been driven into his neck under sterile conditions. Nor had the sea water in which he had been floating been free of bacteria.

We laid him down on the wardroom table. In one hand I had a hemostat. A Pharmacist's Mate stood next to me, hemostats in both hand. I fastened a toothed surgical clamp on the protruding end of wood and gently started pulling. My patient lay, eyes tightly shut, his lips compressed to a thin line. For half a minute the wood didn't budge. I tugged a little harder, lifting the young man's head off the table. Another quarter-inch of the wood appeared at the skin margin. I stopped and inspected. So far, no bleeding except for oozing in the skin around the edge of the wood. I pulled again and now the wood came out more freely. I was amazed at the length of the fragment. Suddenly, it was out. All out. I stood over the wound with my hemostat poised, a gauze pack in my other hand, ready for an eruption. A trickle of blood came from the wound which was now an empty cavity. Miraculously, the wood had passed around every important structure.

The young man opened his eyes. "Is—is it out?"

I nodded.

His voice was hoarse. For the first time during the entire ordeal, his eyes glistened with tears. "Thanks, doc."

In the many years I practiced medicine, I don't think I've had a more grateful patient. Although he didn't know it, he will never have a more relieved doctor.

Several hours later, we moved alongside one of the cruisers in our echelon and transferred all of those we had pulled out of the water.

I later learned there had been twenty survivors, eight of them wounded. Eleven were missing. I felt I'd earned my pay that day.

Chapter 36

The Pacific War reached closer to the Japanese homeland when, on 1 April 1945, Easter Sunday, *Russell* along with more than 1,300 ships with 182,000 troops arrived at Okinawa for the next, and what turned out to be the final phase of the three and one-half year conflict.

For several weeks prior to the landing, ships and planes had bombarded the beach in the vicinity of Naha, capital of the island. Okinawans called the assault a "storm of steel."

While the actual landing was unopposed, the amphibious force had been subjected to Kamakaze attacks from the air as well as from the hundreds of suicide boats and swimmers.

Transports, because of their large size were the most frequent target of the Kamakaze planes, but even the smaller vessels were not immune. The day after the start of the invasion, *Russell* had her closest call. A suicide plane approached from the stern, but with all *Russell's* guns trained on it, the plane was hit dead on and crashed just short of the ship. Another proof of *Russell's* ability to survive while all around her ships were not as fortunate.

The Japanese began using a newer weapon, a Baka bomb adapted from the German pilotless missiles or "buzz bombs." The difference was that the Baka was guided by a pilot. At Okinawa, the missiles were hidden in hillside caves and launched on narrow gauge tracks. One Baka flew at an elevation of about 30 feet over the bow of *Russell* and disappeared over the horizon. No determination was ever made of its target, or if it actually struck anything. *Russell* retaliated by shelling the hillside to close off the tunnel. Several cruisers were called in and added their ordnance to the bombardment. No other Baka appeared from that particular area, attesting to the effectiveness of the gunfire.

A large number of Kamikazes launched from the southern Japanese islands headed for the landing beaches on Okinawa. In order to warn the U.S. troops of the approach of enemy planes, a line of destroyers formed an arc between Japan and Okinawa. It was called a "picket line" probably someone's version of a picket fence. *Russell* was assigned Picket Station One, one of two stations closest to the Japanese mainland. While the concept was good, the Kamakazi pilots found that they didn't need to travel all the way to the beachhead since inviting targets, namely, the ships of the picket line, served their purpose. As a consequence, the casualty rate of picket line ships was extraordinarily high. Over the course of the Okinawa campaign lasting about two months, thirty-four allied ships and craft of all types had been sunk, mostly by Kamikazes, and 368 ships and craft damaged. The fleet had lost 763 aircraft. Total American casualties in the operation numbered over 12,000 killed, including nearly 5,000 Navy dead and almost 8,000 Marine and Army dead and 36,000 wounded. Navy casualties were tremendous, with a ratio of one killed for one wounded as compared to a one to five ratio for the Marine Corps.

Once again, *Russell* showed her invincibility (or luck?) in not suffering a scratch from enemy attacks while all around her picket ships were being sunk or damaged.

The same could not be said of *Russell's* machinery. Age and lack of time to rest and repair damaged parts were taking their toll. It became a game of "whack-a-mole"— fix one thing, something else would break down. The crew made bets on which would end first: the *Russell* or the war.

On 12 April the crew of *Russell* was shocked by the news that President Roosevelt had suffered a fatal stroke at Warm Springs, Georgia. Roosevelt was 63. Although his wan and drawn appearance had been evident for some time, it had been attributed to the strain of the war. The true state of his health, his high blood pressure, had been kept a secret.

Survivor

The crew mustered on deck as the flag was dipped to half staff. With their heads bowed, they listened to Captain Wicks' prayerful words. The mood was somber as everyone went about his duties.

More than one crew member had voiced concern that Vice-President Harry Truman was to be our Commander-In-Chief. Little was known about him since Roosevelt had been such a dominant figure and Truman had been shoved to the background.

Three days after the crew members had mourned President Roosevelt's death, their mood was elevated when, while the ship was on picket patrol, *USS Stack,* another destroyer, came alongside to deliver mail. Even more importantly, they had on board a passenger to be transferred to *Russell*. Lieut. (MC) Fredrick Rosendahl was reporting "to relieve Lieut. (MC) Barry Friedman as Medical Officer." After almost two years aboard *Russell*, I was being relieved to return to the States for further duty. Well, not quite yet. Since we were still on picket station, there was nowhere to go—and swimming was not an option.

But first, we had to get Fred Rosendahl aboard. I scanned the skies praying that no Kamakazi attack was imminent. A Boatswain's Chair was rigged and while I watched with trepidation, he was hauled over the water between the two ships. Once he was safely aboard, I greeted him with a firm handshake and an even firmer hug.

Barry Friedman

Fred Rosendahl was a likeable young man who had been called to active duty from an Orthopaedic Surgery residency in Minneapolis/St. Paul. "I'd been chasing *Russell* all over the Pacific for the past month," he said. "I even had to look for her in Australia and New Zealand."

Su-u-re. I was so glad to see him that I could forgive his taking a pleasure excursion under the pretense of searching for us.

Now *Russell* had the luxury of two medical officers while we waited for another destroyer to take our picket station.

Meanwhile, the daily Kamakaze visits continued giving Fred the opportunity of witnessing the suicide pilots diving into whichever vessel got in its path. When I told him that this had been going on for the past several months, he wondered how *Russell* had escaped when most of her sister ships had been sunk or badly damaged. He gazed at the intact hull and superstructure. "Does this ship have some kind of immunity the others don't have?"

"I hope so," I said. "And for your sake I hope the immunity lasts.

Finally, after two nail-biting weeks, *Russell* was relieved from her picket station and anchored at Kerama Retto, a small island just off the coast of Okinawa. The sea was calm enough so that a motor whaleboat could be lowered. With my sea bag slung over my shoulder, an egg-sized lump in my throat, I tossed a salute to the OOD and, for the last time a salute to the ship's ensign, and with a wave to

Survivor

the crew, my "Band of Brothers" who stood at the rail, I boarded the motor whaleboat.

The boat took me to Kerama Island from where I hitched a ride on another small boat to Naha harbor on the main Okinawa island. There was no place to stay in Naha which was in shambles from the pre-invasion shelling, so I found my way to the airfield which appeared to be a field of shell holes. No planes. I found the Officer in Charge, an Army Captain, in a tent at one end of the field.

"I need to catch a plane to Pearl Harbor," I said.

He looked at me and grinned. "You'd better book another airline, buddy. We haven't secured the field yet."

A mortar shell exploded somewhere on the field and we both flinched. "See what I mean," he said.

I saw what he meant. "I guess I'll just have to wait."

He shrugged. "Unless you want to knock out the gun they just fired."

I told him I didn't do gun emplacements—or machine gun nests.

He directed me to a tent where I hunkered down with a sergeant until the following afternoon by which time someone else had taken out the mortar.

Just before sundown, a plane bumped down on the field, a hospital plane. Shortly afterward several ambulances rolled up and transferred patients on stretchers to the plane. I climbed aboard and the

Barry Friedman

big plane took off. I worked my way out of the war zone starting IVs and changing blood-soaked dressings until we landed in Guam.

From there I caught a Matson Liner which had been converted to a troop carrier, to Honolulu. Although I was leaving the Pacific War Theater, like the other military people I met on my way back to the States, I viewed this as a temporary reprieve. I fully expected I'd be back for the invasion of the Japanese mainland.

Meanwhile, back at the *Russell* Dr. Rosendahl had his baptism of fire the day after he assumed his duties as Medical Officer. A low-flying Kamikaze was spotted closing the ship. Flying through flak, it skimmed over *Russell's* bridge and slammed in the *USS Pinkney*, a hospital evacuation ship full of Army and Marine troops who had been wounded in the Okinawa ground fighting. An explosion rocked the ship and the after-end of the superstructure was walled by a sheet of flame. Water lines, electrical conduits, and steam pipes ruptured. The crew immediately formed rescue and damage control parties. All wards in the amidships hospital area were burned out killing most of the patients.

Russell, along with rescue tugs and landing craft moved in to assist in fire fighting, but the flames continued for another three hours, by which time USS *Pinkney* had lost 18 of her crew and had taken on a heavy list to port. The ship remained afloat, however, and although severely crippled managed to crawl to Saipan for temporary repairs.

Survivor

For the next month, *Russell* alternated between screening jeep aircraft carriers during flight operations, and manning picket stations between mainland Japan and Okinawa.

For some time now the crew had settled into what could only be described as routine duties. Frequent sonar contacts indicated that submarines still operated in the area. Kamakazi plane sightings still brought calls to General Quarters. But after three years in combat, activities that had earlier raised hackles on the necks of crew members now were looked upon as minor inconveniences rather than major events. It's easy to see how bearing witness to so much death and destruction whether on land, in the air or on the sea, can blunt one's sensitivity to such horrors.

One event during the latter days of the Pacific War roused everyone aboard *Russell* from apathy. On 7 May 1945 Germany surrendered unconditionally. The jubilation of the crew was tempered only by the realization that they still had a war to fight.

Although I was miles from the ship having skipped and hopped to San Francisco, on that May morning I boarded a DC3 to the east coast on my final leg home. Although it was a commercial airliner, almost all the passengers were military.

When we were over Omaha, the plane captain announced that Germany had surrendered. The news was expected, so the celebration didn't last long. Most of us expected to be back in the Pacific to the war we had left.

Barry Friedman

We approached New York at dusk and the plane captain announced that he would fly over the Statue of Liberty. He said that we might not be able to see it in the darkness that was coming on, because the light in Liberty's torch had been blacked out since the start of the war. We all crowded to the windows hoping to catch a glimpse of the statue. The next few moments were a once-in-a-lifetime experience. As we gazed down in the gloom, the statue first appeared as a dark mass. From the torch in Lady Liberty's raised hand, a tiny lamp began to glow. At first it seemed no brighter than a match. Gradually it became brighter and brighter — like a huge white flower opening until it lit up the sky. The Statue of Liberty torch, dark through the years of the war, was turned on again. It was VE Day, Victory In Europe.

If there's a point to this story it's this: To those of us returning from the battlefield, the Statue of Liberty that we crawled over each other in our anxiety to see was a symbol that stood for why we had gone to war. So many of our friends, comrades,and loved ones, had died protecting that symbol, assuring that the torch in Liberty's hand would remain bright to light up our lives, our country, our world, our planet.

Chapter 37

On 31 May, *Russell* hampered by frequent breakdowns was ordered back to Pearl Harbor for a patch-up that would carry her through the rest of the war. When it became apparent that the needed repairs were too much for even Pearl Harbor, she turned around, and steamed out of the harbor headed for Puget Sound, Washington.

The elated crew stood at the rail as *Russell* steamed through the Strait of Juan de Fuca to touch the continental United States for what turned out to be her last voyage.

While she was in dry dock at Todd Shipyards a skeleton crew relieved those on leave and headed for home, parents, wives, and sweethearts. On 6 August 1945 the world entered the Nuclear Age with the atomic bombing of Hiroshima, Japan.

While the Western World rejoiced, the remnants of the indescribable destruction in Japan continued to hang on to their faith in their Emperor. Somehow he would get them through all of this.

Two days later, U.S. planes dropped leaflets on Nagasaki warning that they were to be the next atomic bomb victim. When the Japanese warlords signaled their refusal to surrender unconditionally, the Allies kept their promise and unleashed the second and last nuclear device.

Japan's surrender on 15 August undoubtedly saved the lives of countless individuals on both sides. President Truman, who made the decision to use the atomic bomb, stated that he had been advised by some military leaders that the number of American casualties the United States would suffer in a mainland invasion of Japan could be as high as one million.

The Japanese code of *bushido*—"the way of the warrior"—was deeply ingrained. Each soldier was provided with a strict code: never be captured, never break down, and never surrender. Surrender was dishonorable. Each soldier was trained to fight to the death and was expected to die before suffering dishonor. Defeated Japanese leaders preferred to take their own lives in the painful samurai ritual of *seppuku (hara kiri)*. Warriors who surrendered were not deemed worthy of regard or respect.

The men of the *Russell* witnessed firsthand the Japanese determination to die rather than be captured when they attempted to rescue survivors of the destroyer they had sunk off Manila Bay.

The debate over the use of the bomb has continued to the present day. Winston Churchill in a speech before the House of Commons in August 1945 summed up the argument:

Survivor

"There were those who considered that the atomic bomb should never have been used at all. I cannot associate myself with such ideas...I am surprised that very worthy people—but people who in most cases had no intension of proceeding to the Japanese front themselves—should adopt a position that rather than throw this bomb we should have sacrificed a million American and a quarter of a million British lives."

On 15 September Captain Wicks turned over command of *Russell* to Lieut. Commander L.C. Winters, USN. The decision to decommission the ship had already been made and was carried out on 15 November. The charmed *Russell* had survived the war. Through sixteen major engagements none of her crew was killed by enemy guns. The three deaths that occurred on board were survivors of *Hornet* who had been rescued by *Russell*. Two had sustained their injuries when the carrier was bombed, the third was hit by bullets from a plane that strafed *Russell*.

Once out of commission, the *Russell* was sold for scrap.

Barry Friedman

Epilogue

Like the mythical Phoenix, a bird that lives a long life, and then is consumed by flames, only to immediately rise again from the ashes, a new ship bearing the name *Russell* has emerged. Through the lobbying efforts of former "old" *Russell* crew members: Robert Meier, Robbie Robinson, Harris "Red" Austin, Dr. Bob Schmidt, Wallace Thomas, and Bob Meier's daughter, Mrs. Julie Meier Wright, the Navy agreed to build an Arleigh Burke class Aegis guided missile destroyer and name her *USS Russell (DDG-59.)* The "new" *Russell* was commissioned 20 May 1995, Commander (now Vice Admiral) Peter H. Daly, USN in command.

Survivor

References

(Internet Sources)

Aleutian campaign
www.historynet.com/battle-of-the-aleutian-islands-recapturing-attu.htm

Bataan Death March
www.pbs.org/wgbh/amex/macarthur/sfeature/bataan_capture.html
en.wikipedia.org/wiki/Bataan_Death_March
www.eyewitnesstohistory.com/bataandeathmarch.htm

Battle of Guadalcanal
en.wikipedia.org/wiki/Guadalcanal_Campaign
www.historylearningsite.co.uk/battle_of_guadalcanal.htm
en.wikipedia.org/wiki/Naval_Battle_of_Guadalcanal
www.history.army.mil/brochures/72-8/72-8.htm

Battle of Java Sea
www.microworks.net/pacific/battles/java_sea.htm
en.wikipedia.org/wiki/Second_Battle_of_the_Java_Sea

Battle of the Coral Sea
en.wikipedia.org/wiki/Battle_of_the_Coral_Sea
www.historylearningsite.co.uk/battle_of_coral_sea.htm
militaryhistory.about.com/od/worldwari1/p/coralsea.htm
www.microworks.net/pacific/battles/coral_sea.htm
www.worldwar2history.info/Coral-Sea/

Battle of Leyte Gulf
www.angelfire.com/tm/odyssey/LEYTE_GULF_Summary_of_the_Battle_.htm

Barry Friedman

militaryhistory.about.com/od/worldwari1/p/leytegulf.htm

www.microworks.net/pacific/battles/leyte_gulf.htm

www.battle-of-leyte-gulf.com/blg_synopsis/Strategy/strategy.html

Battle of Midway

en.wikipedia.org/wiki/Battle_of_Midway

www.history.navy.mil/photos/events/wwii-pac/midway/midway.htm

militaryhistory.about.com/od/worldwari1/p/Midway.htm

ehistory.osu.edu/wwii/articles/midway/0003.cfm

Battle of Okinawa

en.wikipedia.org/wiki/Battle_of_Okinawa

www.globalsecurity.org/military/facility/okinawa-battle.htm

nisei.hawaii.edu/object/io_1149316185200.html

Battle of Rennell Island

www.historynet.com/battle-of-rennell-island-setback-in-the-solomons.htm

www.battlesforguadalcanal.com/Story/Battles/Rennell_Islands/rennell_islands.html

Battle of Santa Cruz

en.wikipedia.org/wiki/Battle_of_the_Santa_Cruz_Islands

Made in the USA
Lexington, KY
04 June 2017